NORTH

NORTH

**also: Soldiers
Act of Union
Mary's Men**

four plays by

Seamus Finnegan

**Marion Boyars
London · New York**

Published in Great Britain and the United States
in 1987 by Marion Boyars Publishers
24 Lacy Road, London SW15 1NL
26 East 33rd Street, New York. N.Y. 10016

Distributed in the United States by
Kampmann & Co, New York

Distributed in Canada by
Book Center Inc, Montreal

Distributed in Australia by
Wild and Woolley, Glebe, N.S.W.

All performing rights of these plays are strictly reserved and
application for performance should be made to
Patricia MacNaughton, MLR Ltd,
200 Fulham Road, London SW10 9PN

No performance of the plays may be given unless a licence has
been obtained prior to rehearsals.

British Library Cataloguing in Publication Data
Finnegan, Seamus
  North: four plays.
  I. Title   II. Finnegan, Seamus. Act of
  union   III. Finnegan, Seamus. Mary's men
  IV. Finnegan, Seamus. Soldiers
  822'.914   PR6056.1518/

Library of Congress Cataloging in Publication Data
Finnegan, Seamus, 1949—
  North; also, Act of union; Mary's men; Soldiers.
  1. Belfast (Northern Ireland) — Drama.   I. Title:
North.
PR6056.15188A6   1987   822'.914   87-6551

ISBN 0-7145-2870-6 Original Paperback Edition

Typeset in 10/11r Times and Helvetica
by Ann Buchan (Typesetters), Middlesex

Printed and bound in Great Britain by
Biddles Ltd, Guildford and King's Lynn

FOR JULIA

ACKNOWLEDGEMENTS

I would like to thank *Julia Pascal*, the director of these four plays, for her courage and artistry in producing them on the London stage.

I would like to thank *Marion Boyars* for publishing this volume. Now, at least, they can be read in Belfast and Ireland.

SEAMUS FINNEGAN

CONTENTS

FOREWORD

Some of the people who influenced, however indirectly, the writing of these four plays are dead. This volume is partly a memorial to them.

Paddy Murray, whose public house, The Bowling Green, (long since demolished) in York Street, Belfast, provided me with the setting for ACT OF UNION. I'd also like to mention Paddy's son, Jimmy, a school friend, whose experience as victim of an assassination attempt (he survived) I recreate in the play.

Frank McGuiness, a young man of 17 years, lived in the same street as I did in Belfast. On the morning of internment in August 1971, I passed by him. That evening he was dead. Shot by the British Army. Marilyn, the English journalist in SOLDIERS describes the spot where he was murdered.

Pat Poland, the father of another school friend, throughout the sixties and early seventies, provided open house to a group of us where debate and argument lasted long into many nights and mornings. NORTH has provoked much controversy and debate. Pat Poland, I think, would have enjoyed the controversy and disagreed, naturally, with many of the ideas in the play.

Bauxy Drummond, in ACT OF UNION and SOLDIERS has become Bucksey. I first encountered him when he was a barrow-boy. My father pointed him out to me in Castle Lane, Belfast and told me how Bauxy had once played for the reserve team of Belfast Celtic. I met him again when, as a 16 year old member of the Legion of Mary, I helped serve tea in Dover St. hostel for the 'down and outs' who lodged there. Mr. Drummond died, 'a casualty of war' when a car bomb planted by the IRA exploded near the Belfast docks.

Terence Burns, a cousin, gave me my first theatre memory. He played Lord Castlereagh in an amateur production at St Mary's Hall, Bank Street in the mid-fifties. One of Belfast's many 'unsung Miltons', he is 'my cousin the artist' that Banker Joe remembers in MARY'S MEN. The two water colours referred to, of the Antrim Coast Road and Glenavy Falls, Terence Burns painted. They still hang in my parents' Belfast Home.

SOLDIERS

A play in 19 scenes
Can be performed with 4 actors
(doubling/trebling)

SOLDIERS was first produced in October 1981 at the Old Red Lion Theatre Club, London, and transferred to the York & Albany Theatre Club.

CAST

MARILYN/UNBORN CHILD	Christina Schofield
KEVIN/BILLY/DAVID/MAN	Philip Fox
CIARAN/TERRY/BUCKSEY	Sam Dale
ROBERT/YAP	Derek Thompson

Other parts played by the company.
The play was directed by Julia Pascal.

CHARACTERS

MARILYN
KEVIN
CIARAN
BILLY
ROBERT
BUCKSEY
YAP
TERRY
DAVID

A PRIEST
A SOLDIER
2 I.R.A. VOLUNTEERS
S.B. MAN
AN UNBORN CHILD

PROLOGUE

Lights down. Blackout.
Music: Bodhran drum, loud.
Enter cast. Take positions.
Lights up.
Actors prepare the priest in vestments of the Mass. Actors take positions as at the beginning of Mass — priest and congregation.
Cut music. Hear altar bells.
Priest kisses 'altar'. Turns to audience. Raises arms. Makes the sign of the Cross.

PRIEST: In the Name of the Father and of the Son and of the Holy Ghost. Amen.

Music: Gregorian chant. Blackout. Cut music.

1 | SCENE

We see Marilyn (an English journalist). Holding notebook and pen.

MARILYN: 15th August, 1969. Just after 5 p.m. Standing outside
St Comgall's Roman Catholic Primary School. Opposite
Percy Street. A street off the Lower Falls Road in Belfast,
Northern Ireland. Witnessed rioting all day. Catholics and
Protestants. Mainly young men. Some girls helped to
stockpile stones, bricks and bottles. Police and 'B' Specials,
the forces of 'law and order', stood in front of Protestants.
Facing Catholic youths. Sometimes threw stones and bricks
in direction of Catholics. Aided periodic charges by
Protestants. When Catholics counter-attacked Police and
'B' Specials closed ranks to ensure safety of Protestants.
This continued until late afternoon. It was a warm day.
Rumours amongst Catholics that Protestants wanted to
attack and burn down St Peter's church in nearby Derby
Street, the Catholic Pro-Cathedral in Belfast. Also
rumoured that last night a group of men occupied St.
Comgall's school. They had one old Thompson sub-
machine gun. No other fire weapons were said to be
available. A fire is raging in the grain mill opposite. And
another in Andrews' car showrooms. 100 yards to my left.
Houses are gutted in Percy Street and all along the row of
shops and premises to my right. Leading to Divis Street.
People passing me as they walk home from work. They are
directed into the maze of side-streets that run off the Falls
Road by two young men. One of whom told me that a
Protestant sniper was on the roof of a building opposite in
Northumberland Street. Northumberland Street leads
onto the Shankill Road. Protestant. As I look up Percy

Street from outside St Comgall's school the charred shell of a Belfast Corporation bus marks the dividing line of that earlier battle between Catholics, Protestants, Police and 'B' Specials. It is strangely quiet. An eeriness has descended to encompass the whole area. Percy Street and all around smoke rises like incense on an everlasting ritual.

Enter Soldier. Music: Bodhran drum.

A figure has emerged from behind that smouldering Corporation bus. He is dressed in khaki. Battle dress. He carries a rifle. Bayonet drawn. He is young. Pale. Perhaps no more than seventeen. Hesitant and anxious in step. Others like him appear. They come nearer. Nearer. In formation. The British Army is here.

Soldier approaches audience. Drumming loud.

Blackout.

SCENE 2

Sound of altar bells. Spot on Priest.

PRIEST: My dear people, as you all know the British Army is in our midst. It is here, my dear people, to give us respite from our troubles. To relieve us from the worries, anxieties and dangers we Catholics have been living in over the past months. Yes, there are English soldiers here on Irish soil, one might say AGAIN. But let me say this to you my dear people . . . they are here, this time, to PROTECT US! Our Father who art in Heaven hallowed be thy name. . .

Music: drum. Slow beat.

Blackout.

3 SCENE

We see Ciaran and Kevin. They have just returned from demonstration/riot in protest against the killing of 13 people by British paratroopers: Bloody Sunday. Jan. 1972. (Placards, flags, banners).

KEVIN: Some turn-out for the demonstration, eh? There must have been close on 10,000 people there. And wasn't it a quare good riot, Ciaran? Christ, there's nothing like a good riot. 'A fitting end to any march or demonstration'. You know, it's funny, but there are times in the middle of a riot when sometimes I seem to be outside of myself . . . as if I'm watching it all going on. I'm clodding away like a good 'un, running up, taking aim, and jumping for joy if one of the bricks just sneaks over the riot shield of some Brit and gets him between the eyes, and at the same time I'm watching it all. It's like two armies — one of them in khaki (the Brits) and the other in denim — grouping and regrouping for the final assault. I tell you it reminds me of wee Dwyer's Latin lessons when he used to draw those diagrams on the blackboard . . . all about the Romans and the Gauls. Do you remember, Ciaran? Jesus, do I love the smell of a riot! It's like . . . it's like feeling free. Do you know what I mean, Ciaran? It's like this sense of freedom takes hold of you. Must be a bit like the feeling you get when you take certain kinds of drugs. What d'ye think, Ciaran?

CIARAN: I think you're talking through your arse again, Kevin. That's what I think. In fact, I'm not so sure you're not on some kind of drugs.

KEVIN: (*Mock sign of Cross*) 'I swear to God, Mother, I never touched the baby aspirin. It wasn't me! Honest! It wasn't!' (*Pause*) No, but seriously, Ciaran, I was only comparing it. I mean, do you never get that kind of feeling I was talking about in a riot? It's like a . . . like a . . .

CIARAN: A fuck!

KEVIN: Jesus! That's it. Do you know, maybe you've got something there, Ciaran. You know, I never thought of it like that before, but now that you come to mention it. . .

CIARAN: Aye. Well, before you start counting the number of substitute orgasms you've had these past few years, will you shut the fuck up till we hear the news.

(*News bulletin. Tells of burning of British Embassy in Dublin*).

KEVIN: Jesus Christ! Fuckin' hell! The Brit Embassy in Dublin. God, I didn't think they had it in them down there.

CIARAN: Oh, don't worry, I wouldn't get too excited thinking the revolution has come. If I know anything about 'yer men' in the 26 counties, they'll burn it down today, be queueing up for the jobs to rebuild it tomorrow. You wait and see. Oh, they're good at gestures down there! Remember Jack Lynch's 'gesture' in '69 . . . sends troops up to the border and says 'we shall not stand idly by'. One speech from him and the whole so-called 'Irish Republic' is rooted to the spot!

KEVIN: Aye, I know that. But it's not just Dublin. The whole bloody country is up in arms and having demonstrations and marches and riots. Dundalk. Cork. Galway. Limerick. I mean, this is something different, Ciaran. You must admit.

CIARAN: Aye. Maybe. But you can march and demonstrate and even 'feel free' in a riot — so what? So fuckin' what, Kevin? It was a march that those 13 dead bodies were on. But it didn't stop the Paras going in and meaning business now, did it?

KEVIN: But they can't shoot us all, Ciaran. They can't mow us all down. The people on the streets is power, Ciaran. We've always said that. We KNOW that!

CIARAN: And a lot of fuckin' good they are on the streets with both arms the one length. And who says they can't mow us all down. This is the British Army we have here in Northern Ireland, y'know, not the boy scouts! What makes you think they're going to be any different here than they've been anywhere else? Aden, Cyprus, the list is endless! But you think they're going to be kinder to the Paddies, do you?

KEVIN: I didn't say that, Ciaran. But the situations are different — you've got to admit that. They can't just go in and wipe out areas like they did in Cyprus or Aden or wherever.

CIARAN: Well, you tell that to the 13 dead lying up in the mortuary. Tell them that the Paras on Sunday didn't really mean to shoot them. Tell them that the crack regiment of the British Army, the no-messing-about boys, were really just playing at manoeuvres. That it was really just a game like the fuckin' Romans and Gauls on wee Dwyer's fuckin' blackboard. . .

KEVIN: Oh, for fuck's sake, catch yourself on Ciaran, and don't be so fuckin' ridiculous! Blind emotionalism is certainly not the answer. Nobody's denying the thirteen. But we've got to try and see things. . .

CIARAN: . . . 'in perspective' is it, Kevin? In fuckin' perspective? No, comrade, you're the one who's being ridiculous, for if you think that by organizing yet another demonstration, arranging yet another march, even having a full blooded orgasmic riot, you're going to change anything, you'd better 'go on' the drugs immediately. We've tried those ways, Kevin — they've tried them all over the fuckin' world — and oh, yes, they'll let you exercise your democratic rights, they'll let you march up and down like bloody King Cole — but just as soon as you look like getting a little too big for your boots — or your demands become just a little unbearable and they realize that what you're really after is their power — then out comes the big hammer to smash all those little marching citizens on the head. Out come the Paras, Kevin. And it's as plain as plain to see you can't 'demonstrate' against a Para . . . now can you, Kevin. . .? (*Pause*) So. . .?

Both freeze. Take positions to watch Priest. Sound of altar bells. Spot on Priest.

PRIEST: . . . these same people, my dear people, that we see today on the streets of our beloved city, protesting, marching, demonstrating, rioting, using VIOLENCE, my dear people, are the same people the EXACT SAME PEOPLE, that I saw in the 1930's at Hyde Park corner. Plying their ungodly wares. They are not new or different, but the self-same agitators — for I have seen their faces — COMMUNISTS! My dear people. COMMUNISTS! Hail Mary, full of Grace, the Lord is with Thee. . .

Cut. Blackout.

SCENE   4

Sound of Big Ben. We see Robert and Billy (English). In the changing rooms of an amateur football club. Both are in late teens. They are getting 'kitted out' for football match.

BILLY: So you're really going to go through with it, Rob?

ROBERT: Yep. Signed the papers today, didn't I? No backin' out now, mate. It's done. AND I'm really looking forward to it.

BILLY: Rather you than me, mate. That's all I can say. You know, Rob, I can't understand why you're doing it? I mean the Army. The fuckin' army! That means rules and regulations, you know. Taking orders. Do this. Do that. And you're looking forward to THAT. Jesus. It'll just be like being at school again. And you were dead keen on that set-up weren't you?

ROBERT: Rubbish, mate. It's nothing like school.

BILLY: Isn't it? From where I stand it looks too bloody familiar. Worse in fact. There's no easy half-hour detentions in that outfit for misbehaving. Get in trouble with the authorities there, mate, and it's your balls they're after. Not have you written those 100 fuckin' lines?

ROBERT: (*Laughing*) Don't be so fuckin' ridiculous, Billy. You've got some fuckin' weird ideas, mate, about how things work. And you're dead wrong on this one. O.K. So there's a bit of discipline: so maybe that's no bad thing.

BILLY: Oh yeh?

ROBERT: Yeh. So long as there's a purpose to it. You're doing it for something. To achieve something. Not just because some wanker of a teacher tells you to.

BILLY: And you think the Sgt. Major is going to explain nicely to you WHY you are to lick his fat arse? (*Robert just laughs*) So what is it you're going to achieve, then? Eh? Go on, tell us what is the purpose of it?

ROBERT: A job, mate. A fuckin' job for one thing. Money. You know. Skilled trade. Something I can use if and when I leave the Army. Travel. Bit of adventure. Physical fitness. Meet people. See places. Sense of purpose. Loads of things, mate. You wanna nip down the Army Information Centre sometime.

BILLY: I have done.

ROBERT: You have? When?

BILLY: One time we went from school with the careers bloke. I tell you, it scared the shit out of me! I remember, we went in and there was nobody about. Just this display section full of fuckin' dummies dressed like something out of Dr. Who, and mechanical gadgets with minds of their own which were capable of all sorts of wonderful fuckin' feats beyond the understanding of ordinary men. I tell you, mate, those fuckin' contraptions were the only things in that office that looked like they didn't take orders. (*Robert is hysterical with laughter*) Oh, you can laugh, mate. But it wasn't fuckin' funny. One teacher and 15 C.S.E. school boys just standing there in the middle of the floor, surrounded by these monsters — and not a human face in sight. Just silence. And then all of a sudden one of these fuckin' gadgets, all arms and legs and making Dalek noises, starts walking towards us. Well I can tell you, mate, that the British Army scored nil on that little recruitment exercise. And the careers master, poor bugger, was absent from school for 3 days after it!

Robert, bent over with laughter, recovers.

ROBERT: Well, it's too late to tell me all this now, Billy. The job's done. I report to the Centre next Tuesday morning. But I'll be on the look-out for those gadgets.

BILLY: Yeh, you do that, mate. But I tell you, they're probably friendlier than some of . . .

ROBERT: O.K. So it might be hard in some ways. But it's a good life for a man. My dad always says that the years he spent in the army were the best days of his life. And that was during the war, which was no fuckin' picnic. But he doesn't regret it. Not a fuckin' minute of it. He's still got friends that he met then.

BILLY: Aye. Maybe. Well, the best of British luck to you, mate, and thanks for the offer but I think I'll just stick around here in civvy street and wait for you to come back and tell what it's like in your part of Heaven.

ROBERT: You're not going to even THINK about signing up then, Billy?

BILLY: The only signing I'll do'll be on the dole. Regular like, 10.00 a.m. every other Thursday. Unless, of course, Terry Neill hears that I'm ten times better than Liam Brady.

ROBERT: And what sort of life is that?

BILLY: Not much. But it is a LIFE.

ROBERT: Eh?

BILLY: You mean you haven't thought about it?

ROBERT: Thought about what, for Christ's sake?

BILLY: Well, given this great life you're going to be having in Her Majesty's Army, what with all this travel and meeting people and adventure . . . have you ever thought about what happens if instead of being an electrician in Berlin, that Sgt. Major tells you that you're being sent to Northern Ireland? And that's an order, soldier. What happens then, Rob? What the fuck do you do then?

Robert and Billy exchange looks. Freeze.

Music: Gregorian chant. Enter Priest. Priest ceremonially gives Robert rifle and beret. Robert salutes. Priest blesses him. Blackout. Cut music.

5   SCENE

We see Bucksey and Yap, two Belfast 'Winos'. They are both in Hell and drinking poteen.

YAP: (*After a pause, drinking*). You know, Bucksey, I'm really grateful you gave me the wire about this place. Let me know, kinda style.

BUCKSEY: Why's that, Yap?

YAP: Oh, several reasons. But there's one that would have borne considerable consideration even if there weren't the others.

BUCKSEY: And what one's that?

YAP: The drink! (*Bucksey laughs*) Oh, you can laugh, Bucksey. Not that you're one to refuse it when it's offered, yourself.

BUCKSEY: True!

YAP: But I hear that there's only the one sort of liquor in . . . in . . . Heav . . . Heaven.

BUCKSEY: It's alright, Yap. You can say the word. There's no crimes or censorship here in Hell.

YAP: Aye! You know, Bucksey, I couldn't get over it. Imagine, if you'd led a good and perfect life on earth! You might even have been an abstainer, a life-long Pioneer! And you thought that, well, at least when I die and go up to Heaven I'll be able to have a few pints of Guinness and a few half 'uns of whiskey now and again out of St Peter's cocktail cabinet. There you are. You've passed the test and got through the Pearly Gates and it's the first Saturday night and you're sitting waiting with your Guardian Angel and your tongue's hanging out for a drink. . .

BUCKSEY: . . . and St Peter takes out this bloody big bundle of keys and hands it to 'Himself' to open the cabinet. And the whole of Heaven is 'shaking' with bated non-alcoholic breath. . .

YAP: . . . and the key turns and the doors open. And the little angels sing, 'GLORIA IN EXCELSIS' . . . and . . . and. . .

BUCKSEY: And there it is! Rows and rows of bottles stretching all the way to infinity and back. . .

YAP: And not a bloody thing in them but RED ALTAR WINE! (*They both laugh, drinking*) But here, Bucksey. This is a quare drop of poteen.

BUCKSEY: Oh, it's the Devil's own, Yap. I heard that he stole it from the British Authorities after THEY had confiscated it from some of the boys in the Kesh.

YAP: Is that a fact? Oh, more power to his elbow if he stole it from them bastards. You know, I wish that more people in the North of Ireland knew that he was on their side — the Devil, I mean.

BUCKSEY: Aye. I know. But to his eternal glory, the Devil is not what one might call a great lover of the Sassenach.

YAP: Well, that would certainly explain, Bucksey, why there's none too many of the English breed here.

BUCKSEY: And the few that are Yap, it seems they're not English at all. Jews mostly.

YAP: Is that a fact, Bucksey? Jews and Paddies?

BUCKSEY: Sure, didn't I have a great yarn with the Devil himself one day about what the difference was between the English and the Irish?

YAP: You did not, did ye? And what did he say?

BUCKSEY: Oh, I'll tell you now, Yap. But, here, it's a bit of a long story. And this bottle's empty. We'll go and get another one and then we can settle without interruption or anxiety that the drinks going to run out.

YAP: Right, Bucksey. Right. God you've got your head screwed on the right way. Another bottle. And the story. Oh, it must be a powerful story that one. As powerful a one as any seanchai could tell in all the centuries and in all the West!

Both Exit. Blackout.

6   SCENE

MARILYN: (*She speaks into tape recorder*). Spring. 1974. Late afternoon. There is a watery sunshine shining on a street in an estate in Andersontown, Belfast, Northern Ireland. It is quiet. But for the voices of a few children playing in the garden of one of the semi-detached houses. A few are semi-detached. Most are terraced blocks of four or six . . . the 'back to front' houses, as local people call them. The kitchen facing onto the street. Women. Standing washing. Looking out. Or up at the Black Mountain. One of the range of hills that surround the city of Belfast.

A block of shops nearby . . . all but one of the five shops has hardboard where the glass windows used to be. Hardboard makes a good surface for slogan writers. 'Fuck the Brits'. 'Smash internment'. 'A Nation Once Again'. 'Ireland Unfree shall never be at Peace'.

Two boys have just come out of the confectionery shop. The one with the glass windows. They laugh and pull at each other. And run off down the street. Throwing crisps at each other as they go. Not noticing. Not anymore. The 'shrine'. Opposite the sweet shop. On the pavement there is the dark red stain of blood. A 17-year old boy died there this morning. Shot by the British Army. The army say he was carrying what 'looked like a rifle'. The local people ask 'where is that rifle'? Beside the red stain on the kerbstone there are two milk bottles. Both empty but for withering bunches of a wild yellow flowers. Beside the bottles are two brass candlesticks. White candles. Long extinguished. Between the candles and bottles is a small plaster statue of Our Lady. Christ's Mother. The Mother of God. When I arrived this morning shortly after the shooting of the boy, I spoke to a young American woman. A student. She was standing in front of this little hastily-erected grotto. There were other women. Local women. Some praying with rosary beads. Others just passing by. Blessing themselves as they went. The young American woman told me that she had last seen such an 'altar shrine' in Africa. Tribesmen had spent some time arranging a shrine at the place of death. The death of a boy. Also shot. Also by an Army.

But it is quiet now, here in this street in Andersontown, Belfast, Northern Ireland. It is growing dark. Making it almost impossible to make out the blood stain on the pavement. A few men returning from work pass by. Pass by the grotto. Not noticing. Not seeing. Not knowing. Their wives will tell them later of whose death came today.

Pause. Music: The Last Post.
Enter two I.R.A. volunteers in dark glasses and with black berets. They are carrying a coffin draped in Tricolour. Stop centre stage. Music stops. Spot on Priest.

PRIEST: Get that Fenian coffin out of my church. OUT! OUT!

Music: Last post. Exit volunteers. Blackout.

SCENE   7

Spot on Ciaran sitting on a chair naked. We hear the footsteps of a man slowly pacing to and fro. They stop. Start again. Stop. Start again. Man approaches Ciaran. Spot off him. The following we hear in a blackout. Sound of Ciaran being struck. Scream.

MAN: Now listen, you fuckin' Irish maniac. We've met your type before. We know how to deal with your kind. We have the experience. (*Spits out words*) And let me tell you, friend, we always win. (*Shouts*) ALWAYS! We don't mess about here. We deliver the goods. We get the answers we want. (*Loud*) WE WANT. Do you understand that, Ciaran? And you know why we ALWAYS win, Ciaran, don't you? (*Pause*) 'Cause WE'RE ENGLISH, Ciaran. ENGLISH, Paddy, ENGLISH! (*Pause*) Now, we're not saying you're an activist, Ciaran. I mean, it's not as if we regarded you as a subversive. (*Laughs*) You could be as innocent as Jesus Christ. (*Laughs. Cut*) But we're not sure either, Ciaran. And we like to be sure about things. Neat and tidy like, Ciaran. You know what I mean? 'Cause we're English, Ciaran. And we like things neat and tidy . . . clean, like, Paddy. (*Pause*) We want to help you, Ciaran. Help your family. Your 'friends'. And you can help us do that, Ciaran. It's easy. Oh so easy. You can help us to help them. The simple stroke of a pen does it, Ciaran. That's all it takes. That's all. (*Manically*) Now sign it, you fuckin' Irish bastard! Sign it. Or I'll have you crawling naked over barbed wire and glass until your prick and balls are like shreds of spaghetti. Sign it, you bastard! Sign it! SOCIETY NEEDS YOU!

Sound of loud scream.

8 SCENE

Spot on Priest. Altar bells.

PRIEST: . . . My dear people, it grieves me to say it. But, though I am measuring my words carefully, I can only say and indeed must say, that in our city today are not decent ordinary soldiers . . . NOT the forces of 'Law and Order'. Is torturing a man law and order? No, my dear people. For some of those that we have in our midst today can only be described as the — SCUM OF ENGLAND!

Spot off. Drumming begins. Slow beat.

SCENE 9

Music. Slow beat of Bodhran drum. An army post in Andersontown, Belfast. The atmosphere is one of fatigue and despair. Enter Robert and Terry and Actress playing Unborn Child. Take positions: Robert lying asleep with Playboy magazine on chest. Terry drinking can of beer. Unborn Child . . . unseen. Shadowy light. Drum stops. Silence.

Sound of short burst of automatic fire.
Pause.
Sound of single rifle shot rings out. Echoes.
Silence.

UNBORN CHILD: You killed me before I was born.

ROBERT: (*In his sleep*) It wasn't my fault.

UNBORN CHILD: I had one month to go. I was doing fine. The doctor said: 'Mother and baby are doing fine' AND YOU SHOT ME.

ROBERT: I'm telling you. It wasn't my fault. Your mother got caught in the cross fire and . . .

UNBORN CHILD: I would have been a girl. My mother and father wanted a girl. But you . . .

ROBERT: It was an accident. We didn't mean to . . . to . . .

UNBORN CHILD: Shoot my mother and kill me. But you DID.

ROBERT: An acc . . . accident . . . it was unavoidable . . . couldn't be helped . . . your mother got caught . . . we just knew we were being fired on. . . We weren't sure where it was coming from. . .

UNBORN CHILD: You KNEW where my pregnant mother was.

ROBERT: No! I mean . . . yes. I saw this woman . . . but things happened so fast . . . we hadn't time to . . . we were under automatic fire.

UNBORN CHILD: And you didn't want to get shot.

ROBERT: It wasn't like that . . . can't you UNDERSTAND?

UNBORN CHILD: UNDERSTAND? Understand that I was shot dead before birth?

ROBERT: How can I explain to you? It's impossible. You were . . . you were . . . 'unfortunate'.

UNBORN CHILD: Unfortunately . . . KILLED.

ROBERT: It was an ACCIDENT . . . a TRAGIC ACCIDENT . . . but it wasn't OUR fault. If anyone's to blame . . . blame those who were shooting at us . . . it's THEY who are your real murderers.

UNBORN CHILD: But it was a bullet from YOUR gun that went through my mother's abdomen into my incomplete body.

ROBERT: Yes. But that bullet would never have been fired if we hadn't been fired at . . . remember. . . THEY started the shooting.

UNBORN CHILD: Who started it means little to me. (*Pause*) Why were THEY shooting at you?

ROBERT: They wanted to kill us.

UNBORN CHILD: Why should they want to kill you?

ROBERT: God alone knows that. But they do. They keep shooting at us.

UNBORN CHILD: Have you done something to them. Are YOU their enemy?

ROBERT: THEY seem to think so. For they have declared war on us.

UNBORN CHILD: WHY? WHY SHOULD THEY DO THAT?

ROBERT: I don't know. I don't understand it all. When we first came THEY seemed happy to see us. But that soon changed.

UNBORN CHILD: WHY did you come in the first place?

ROBERT: I was sent. I am a soldier. I obey orders.

UNBORN CHILD: WHO sent you?

ROBERT: My superiors.

UNBORN CHILD: WHY did they send you?

ROBERT: To keep the peace.

UNBORN CHILD: But you are a SOLDIER.

ROBERT: Yes.

UNBORN CHILD: But aren't soldiers used for fighting?

ROBERT: Yes. But this was different.

UNBORN CHILD: But aren't soldiers trained to kill?

ROBERT: Yes. But that doesn't mean we go round killing ALL the time. This was different. We were sent to keep the peace.

UNBORN CHILD: WHY did you kill ME then?

ROBERT: I've explained about that. It was an accident. We didn't mean to . . . to kill you.

UNBORN CHILD: But you DID.

ROBERT: Yes . . . but . . . but . . . I don't understand all this any more than you do. . .

UNBORN CHILD: I was not given the chance to understand.

ROBERT: Maybe you were . . . lucky.

UNBORN CHILD: LUCKY?

ROBERT: YES. LUCKY!

UNBORN CHILD: Lucky to have been killed before birth?

ROBERT: YES! YES! That way you'll never know about . . . life. That way you'll remain . . . INNOCENT. Better that than not to understand . . . not to . . . know . . . or to know . . . that YOU CAN KILL and not know WHY . . . BETTER NOT TO BE BORN THAN TO BE BORN BUT NOT GIVEN A LIFE.

Silence.

UNBORN CHILD: I had one month to go. I would have been a girl. I was to be called . . . Mary.

As lights slowly fade Terry plays with beer can agitatedly. Enter Priest. Spot follows him round. He is carrying small coffin and wreath on top. He recites 'Hail Mary'. Blackout.

10 SCENE

We see Bucksey and Yap as in scene 5.

YAP: So what did he say, Bucksey? What did he say was the difference between the Irish and the English?

BUCKSEY: Well, he said a number of things. He didn't just come down to one basic difference.

YAP: Bit complicated was it? Set you thinking?

BUCKSEY: Aye. It certainly did that. To tell you the truth, Yap, the more he said the less I understood. Oh it was very complex, Yap. Aye. Complex.

YAP: Well, tell us some of the things he said that you can remember.

BUCKSEY: Well. He said part of it, a big part, was to do with religion.

YAP: Protestants and Catholics!

BUCKSEY: Aye. You could put it that way. But it wasn't that simple.

YAP: What? Because there are some Irish who are Protestants?

BUCKSEY: Oh, he only mentioned them in passing. So far as he was concerned they were Irish.

YAP: He should tell that to Paisley and to them that lives in the North of Ireland.

BUCKSEY: But if you notice, Yap, those that were Protestant in the North of Ireland, here in Hell, they're just Irish, like us.

YAP: You mean it's like when they go to England to work. To the Englishman, we're all PADDIES. They don't distinguish between Protestant Paddy and Catholic Paddy . . . all Paddies!

BUCKSEY: The same thing, Yap. The same thing. More or less. But y'see, Yap, he didn't really talk about the Irish as being Catholics or Protestants.

YAP: He didn't. Hmmm. Oh, you mean there's English Catholics as well?

BUCKSEY: Aye. There is. But he saw them not so much as Catholics but as English.

YAP: Ah, Jesus, you're beginning to confuse me altogether, Bucksey.

BUCKSEY: I'm confusing myself, Yap. I told you it was complex. But let me finish what I was saying.

YAP: I'm listening, Bucksey. I'm listening.

BUCKSEY: I've got it now. I remember.

YAP: What?

BUCKSEY: He said that the big difference, or one of them, was that the Irish were PAGANS and the English weren't.

YAP: Did he indeed? Pagans? And what did he mean by that?

BUCKSEY: No. Not Pagan in the sense that you were told you were a Pagan if you didn't go to Mass on a Sunday.

YAP: Well? What then?

BUCKSEY: But Pagan in the sense that we were before St Patrick came.

YAP: Well, he wasn't an Irishman anyway. You know, I wouldn't be surprised to find out that he was an English agent sent over by the British Crown to try and undermine our Paganism!

BUCKSEY: Well, in a way, there you have it, Yap.

YAP: Have what?

BUCKSEY: Your theory could be right. For it was with his coming that we started on the practice of just having the ONE GOD . . . all that business of the shamrock and three in one. . .

YAP: Why? How many did we have before?

BUCKSEY: Quite a few by all accounts. And the Devil seems to think that that is where we took a wrong turning.

YAP: Oh well, he would say that, wouldn't he?

BUCKSEY: No. You have him wrong there, Yap. For he doesn't like being the one and only Devil either.

YAP: Eh?

BUCKSEY: That's his point you see. He's against this business of one God and one Devil . . . he's all for lots of each.

YAP: He is? But Bucksey, I don't understand. You're getting me confused again . . . and what's all this to do with the difference between the English and the Irish?

BUCKSEY: That's it, Yap. You see, the Devil says that even in spite of St Patrick and this one God lark we still behave and act underneath as if there were lots of them. Gods that is. And Devils.

YAP: It all sounds a bit mumbo-jumbo to me. What's he on about? Magic?

BUCKSEY: Exactly, Yap. Exactly. You see you do understand.

YAP: Do I?

BUCKSEY: That's it. That's it. Magic! We have it and the English don't.

YAP: Don't they? Why not?

BUCKSEY: Because they DO behave as if there is only one God. And one Devil. And what's worse, they think he's an Englishman.

YAP: Who? The Devil?

BUCKSEY: No. God.

YAP: Him? I'm lost. Lost. Lost.

BUCKSEY: And you see, that's where the politics comes in.

YAP: Oh, Jesus. No. Not politics AND religion. Not those two. Not again.

BUCKSEY: But the Devil says that's all there is — politics and religion. And, you see, with the English thinking that God is an Englishman . . . that's where they get their politics from.

YAP: They always did think THEY were the chosen people right enough. But here, Bucksey, if you're going to talk much more (*indicates empty bottle*) we better saunter down to the Devil's kitchen for another bottle of the poteen.

BUCKSEY: Christ, you're right. God, we're getting through it rightly. And isn't it great to know that there's always more. You know, Yap, I pity those poor bastards in Heaven and them stuck with all that fuckin' red altar wine. (*Chants*) Dominus Vobiscum.

YAP: Et cum spiriti tu tuo.

Exit, laughing. Blackout.

INTERVAL

SCENE 11

We see Marilyn speaking into a tape recorder.

MARILYN: November. 1979. Mid-morning. Whiterock Road. White. Rock. Cnoic Ban in the Gaelic. Outside, what was Corrigan Park. A Gaelic games playing field. Now an Army post. High corrugated iron. Barbed wire. Fencing. On the other side of the road, the City Cemetery. For Protestants. There is a Protestant church on the Falls Road. At Broadway. The congregation still comes for services on a Sunday. Despite all, a symbol of Catholic tolerance. Unlikely that such a situation could exist on the Protestant Shankill Road.

The army post. In Corrigan Park. On high ground. Inside, a very high, spire-like structure reaches towards the sky. Attached. Fixed to this aerial is an 'electronic eye'. The eye faces in the direction of Milltown Cemetery. Catholic. The Falls Road and surrounding West Belfast area has always had more than its quota of cemeteries, hospitals and churches. One of the purposes of the electronic eye is to record funerals. Republican funerals at Milltown cemetery. At the Republican plot, that section of the cemetery reserved for those who die for the Irish Republic. It is raining. A wet grey Belfast day. Mist on the Black Mountain. No other rain compares. No other November day can be quite as miserable. Manchester — perhaps. The same greyness. The same constant drenching drizzle.

But Manchester has no army post like this one. In Corrigan Park. No electronic eye keeping watch over the crosses, the tombstones, the already-dead and the about-to-be-buried. I see in my mind the cemetery where I have witnessed the ritual burial of men and women. The quiet mourners whipped and lashed by rain and wind as they stand on the mud and clay adjacent to that six-foot deep hole. I strangely imagine all those dead bodies rising up in one and moving purposefully in the direction of this electronic eye. No stranger, perhaps, than this picture I 'really' do see. This British technological eye — planted on steel feet, in this field where the ancient game of hurling was once played — scanning as it does the ghettoes where Irish Catholics live. Watching. Monitoring. Their lives. And their deaths.

As Marilyn finishes, sound of Bells. Cross-Fade to Priest enacting the 'Consecration' of the Mass. Raising the Host and Chalice . . . to be worked out in rehearsal. Blackout.

12 SCENE

We see Ciaran: a prisoner in Long Kesh. He speaks directly to audience.

CIARAN: Come to visit me, have you? Come to spy on a REAL LIVE IRISH 'TERRORIST'? For we 'Irish Terrorists' are always 'Terrorists'. Always Murderers! There are other kinds of

TERRORISTS. From other parts of the world. But sometimes they're called GUERILLAS or FREEDOM FIGHTERS.
There have even been HOSTAGE TAKERS! (*Sings*) 'But if
you're Irish' . . . YOU'RE A TERRORIST! How's that for
straight talking and no messing? A MURDERER who
commits heinous crimes against society. (*Pause*) And
humanity.

Pause

Mind you, I'm surprised they let you in. They're a bit
choosy who sees this place. You have to be real top-shelf
material to get in here AND leave when you want to. We've
had the odd Government Minister, y'know. But they don't
stay long. Can't stand the smell of what they've made.
Oh, we did have a Bishop the other day. But he didn't stay
long either. Makes a bit of a change from all that incense,
eh? I heard that after he left, he said that conditions in here
weren't fit for animals, never mind human beings. But then
I suppose it's hard for you to know what category to put an
Irish Terrorist in. Mind you, it's even harder for the bishops
for they keep changing their minds. Am I a victim fallen
into sin? Or the Devil himself? Wonderful, isn't is? The
Rock that Peter built swims with the tide. Papal Infallibility
it seems, rests in Westminster, these days.
Though I'm not a practising Catholic myself, as you'll
probably have gathered, I do prefer the traditional Church.
The grand old diehard attitudes, where a principle was a
principle. And if you broke one of them you were beyond
the pale. DAMNED! . . . As the saying goes. At least you
knew where you stood in those days. EXCOMMUNICATED!
It's all this modern Vatican II stuff I can't stand. I mean, the
whole thing smacks of liberal democracy. (*Pause*) Well,
there y'are now, I've said it . . . those terrible words. I
mean, that's one thing about the Brits . . . oh, you think
they have a liberal democracy, do you? Well, right enough I
suppose, the facade is still there and the old Imperial
jackboot isn't worn as often as it used to be . . . it's out of
fashion, so to speak. But against that, the last time there
was a place like this LONG KESH was during the 1930's. In
Germany. Fascism they called it then. Bit extravagant that,
you think? Aye. Well, you're probably right. For there's

none of today's Tories a patch on wee Adolf. They haven't the guts. Still. Maggie's trying. You gotta hand it to her. She's trying.

Pause

I hope yiz aren't misunderstanding me. I'm not complaining. I'm not pleading. I mean, so far as they're concerned I AM THE ENEMY. And I have to be dealt with — one way or the other. I don't blame them for the interrogation or the torture or putting me in here. In fact, putting me in here is only a half measure — you know I'm thinking that maybe that's what liberal democracy is — for if they'd done the job properly, I'D BE DEAD!

Pause

For you see, that's what I want for them . . . DEATH! DEATH, for politicians and bishops! DEATH, to their sick rotten corrupting minds! DEATH, to their imprisonment! And I'm not talking about this place. Only bodies rot and die in here. For our power is that you can't intern our minds. Not in here, you can't. Out there it's easy. But not in here. In here is where FREEDOM is! And like the stench, it's going to spread and erupt and blow them all to fuckin' smithereens.

Blackout

Cross-Fade to Priest.

PRIEST: MURDER IS MURDER! My dear people. The 5th Commandment says: THOU SHALT NOT KILL! THOU . . . SHALT . . . NOT . . . KILL! No cause, no injustice, is ever the justification for the taking of a sacred human life. NEVER! NEVER! THOU SHALT NOT KILL!

Blackout.

We see Robert and Terry in Andersonstown Army Post as in scene 9.
They both look shocked and dazed, particularly Robert.

Silence

ROBERT: What do you think made him do it, like, Terry?

TERRY: 'Cause he was a fuckin' mad bastard, that's why.

ROBERT: But he was always so level headed, Andy was. I mean, of all the guys in this fuckin' regiment Andy must have been one of the coolest. I mean, even when we were out on patrol — under fire — fuckin' explosions, the lot — Andy was always the bloke to look to. I mean, he used to say to me, 'Don't think about it, just do it, kid'.

TERRY: Aye. Well, he shoulda fuckin' remembered his own advice, shouldn't he? Cool guys who don't think about it don't go fuckin' beserk and start firing at their mates in camp. AND singing 'Fuck the Queen'.

ROBERT: Yeh. But why, Terry? Why?

TERRY: Look, mate, if you keep asking why and wondering and thinking about it, you're going to go the same way as that fuckin' lunatic did. Just leave it, mate. Right? Andy's dead. And just be fuckin' grateful we got him before he did any of us. We can do without guys like Andy in this outfit. It's had a fuckin' bad enough effect on some of the lads as it is. Now take my advice and forget it. It's over and done with. We got problems enough in this hell-hole without fuckin' worryin' about the likes of him. That's for them who runs things to worry about. Not for us. It's not our job, mate. O.K.?

Pause

ROBERT: Terry?

TERRY: Yeh?

ROBERT: O.K., I listened to what you said and I see your point.
But . . . but don't you ever think about it?

TERRY: Think about WHAT?

ROBERT: Here. I mean . . .

TERRY: Look, if you're still going to fuckin' go on about Andy and
what happened and why, then you better go and do it
somewhere else, mate, 'cause I'm not listening. Now, give
it a fuckin' rest, will you? (*Throws him a magazine*) Here,
have a look at that, should keep your mind occupied.

ROBERT: I'm not talking about Andy. Though it makes you think,
like. No, I'm not talking about what happened. I mean . . .
I mean, don't you ever think about it at all, Terry? I mean,
why we're here? What we're doing? What it's all for?

TERRY: NO!

ROBERT: Never?

TERRY: NEVER! Now read that fuckin' magazine. And think about
what you're missing. And how many times you're going to
do it when you're on leave.

ROBERT: But Terry, you must do . . . sometimes. . .

TERRY: Look, mate, I've told you. NEVER. At no time. And I
strongly recommend you to keep your mouth shut about it.
Or you'll be landing yourself in trouble.

ROBERT: But. . .

TERRY: Fuckin' hell, mate. O.K. You wanna talk about it? Well,
you listen to me a minute. And think, if thinking is what
you're on about. Think hard on what I fuckin' say. One:
This is the army, mate. Not the fuckin' boy scouts. Two:
You're a soldier. That means you obey orders. Do what
you're told to do. Three: Being a soldier means you fight.
Kill people if necessary. Four: You're not a fuckin'
politician, so you don't wonder — think — about what
country you're in or why. Five: If you don't do what I've
just said, you're a fuckin' lousy soldier and shouldn't be in
the fuckin' army.

ROBERT: But Terry, I can't help fuckin' thinking about it. I think about it more and more. Every time I go out on patrol. Every time I stop some old geezer to search him. Every time I enter one of those fuckin' miserable little houses and look under the floor boards. Every time I run from one street corner to another to another. I'm running but I'm thinking. And the more I do it the more difficult it gets to reach that other street corner. You know, I've nearly felt myself stop dead in the middle of the road and say: 'what am I running for? Why don't I walk?' It's like I'm dreaming — and I keep having this dream, Terry. . .

TERRY: You just do that, mate. And you'll be dreaming for ever. You'll stop dead alright. But it won't be thinking. Or dreaming, that'll have done it. It'll be a sniper's bullet. And what thinking are you going to do when you're lying in the middle of the road . . . your eyes still wide open but you're not seeing anything? And there's blood pouring from your chest and mouth and the 'little people' are doing an Irish jig round your body and clapping their hands and screaming: 'We've killed another squaddie. We've killed another squaddie'. Guys like you really fuckin' piss me off. You shouldn't be in the army. You're not fit for it. Tell me, soldier. What made you join up in the first place? It's not the war. There's no conscription. Not like when your old man had to join. You chose to. You chose it, matey. Why? Go on tell me. Why? Fuckin' tell me. WHY? WHAT WAS YOUR DREAM THEN, SOLDIER?

Slow cross-fade to coffin draped in Union Jack. Priest standing at its head, blessing it as at funeral service. Simultaneous blackout. Spot on Robert: look of horror in direction of coffin. Blackout.

We see Marilyn, the English journalist, and David, Marilyn's editor. They are in David's office. The office of a large British broadcasting corporation.

MARILYN: What the hell do you mean, the programme's not being screened?

DAVID: Just that. I mean it's not being screened. We're putting out that film on Iran in place of it.

MARILYN: But why, for God's sake? Half an hour ago it was all systems go. What the hell has happened to change it?

DAVID: Half an hour is a long time in television, Marilyn. I'm sorry. But that's what I've been 'ordered' to do. Take off the transmission.

MARILYN: By whom?

David smiles and shrugs.

MARILYN: Is that all you're going to do? Smile inanely and shrug your shoulders.

DAVID: There's nothing else I can do, Marilyn. AND there's nothing you can do either.

MARILYN: Oh, we'll see about that. You may be happy to be the whipping boy of the powers that be in this great English Liberal Broadcasting Body, but not me. Not me, David.

DAVID: Oh, come on that's unfair. I've already put my head on the chopping block over this programme. I've fought for it like I've never fought for any other programme.

MARILYN: Well, obviously, not hard enough. When it only takes a phone call from 'on bloody high' not two hours before transmission for you to touch your cap and say 'Yes sir, no sir' without even asking for ANY explanation.

DAVID: None would've been given, Marilyn. Come on, you know that. People in their position, don't HAVE to explain or excuse anything.

MARILYN: Yes, I know. They're so used to TELLING. Well, if that's the way this outfit operates then here's one lady who wants no part in it. They can find some other mug to do their cosy 'CENSORED' programmes about Northern Ireland. IRAN is it? And what the fuck has Iran got to do with Mrs. Smith from Salford, who sees her Squaddie son come home in a red, white and blue box?
This programme was about those that are responsible for sending Mrs. Smith's son back in that box. And why they're doing it. Why? Doesn't Mrs. Smith have a right to know that? Obviously not. Or perhaps Mrs. Smith cares more about the Ayatollah than she does about her son? Iran! Fucking Iran. Christ, will the British do anything rather than look at what's happening in their own backyard? — or rather somebody else's yard that they happen to be occupying? But then that's not news, is it? That's just the way it should be. For what's new about that? They've always occupied some poor bastard's yard.

DAVID: That's a fine impassioned political speech, Marilyn. But let me tell you something . . . even nearer to home. Do you think there'll ever be anyone to tell that story to Mrs. Smith, if YOU RESIGN? For I can guarantee that your job would be filled before I caught the 5.25 from Waterloo tonight — if you resigned. There's always enough worms hiding in the woodwork to step into the role of Yes men or Yes women. And what good will it do? None! All that will happen is that what programmes do get made will be even more mediocre and 'safe' than the ones that get made now. You think I haven't thought about it? You think I just say 'Yes sir, no sir'. Well, that's right. I do! But you name one other programme editor in this lousy Corporation who would even have entertained your proposal, never mind supported it. I can tell you, Marilyn, there isn't one. Not bloody one. And that's why I don't resign and march off in a huff to make independent films nobody but the converted sees anyway. For just as long as I sit in this chair, no one else can. And maybe — just maybe — one of the tricky assignments that I give my blessing to, like yours, Marilyn — like yours — will actually slip through the bureaucratic net and be flickering on the screen before anyone has realized. But the chances of that happening, Marilyn, if I vacate this chair are NIL! And by the same token, if you resign no programme half as risky or controversial will be even thought of, never mind made.

MARILYN: And what does it matter, David? What does it fucking matter? For those that are really worth making and seeing and need to be made and seen never bloody are anyway. We're fooling ourselves, David. No one else. They 'let us' make certain programmes. They let us be 'controversial' 'risky' 'dangerous' 'anti-establishment'. But only where it doesn't matter or count. It's their terms of reference. Their code and they soon nail it on the head if we ever show signs of really being any of those things.

And I wonder sometimes if we ever really were 'dangerous' for if we really were . . . they wouldn't just cancel the transmission of a programme, now would they? For if we were really 'dangerous', or 'anti-establishment' — or 'subversive' — it would be US they'd cancel, David.
They would CANCEL US.

Blackout.

15 SCENE

We see Ciaran and Kevin in a pub. They both look older. The time is the present. We last saw Kevin in scene 3 (1972).

KEVIN: You've ten minutes to get out, comrade, before this place goes up.

Ciaran swings round aggressively. Sees Kevin. Relaxes.

CIARAN: Oh, it's you, is it?

KEVIN: Well, what about you, Ciaran? How are you? I heard you were out. Good to see you. Let me get you a drink. What are you having?

CIARAN: I'll have a pint of Guinness. I'm out about a month. I'm fuckin' awful. And I'll have a Jameson whiskey to go with the Guinness.

Drinks business.

KEVIN: Jesus, mate, you look a bit rough. You look as if you've been celebrating for the whole month you've been out.

CIARAN: Aye. That's right. Celebrating my new found 'freedom'. My hard won 'liberty'.

KEVIN: Christ, it's good to see you, Ciaran. It really is, comrade.

CIARAN: Ah, do me a favour. Drop all that comrade stuff, will ye?

KEVIN: Why? What's up? Don't tell me you've gone and joined the S.D.L.P. since you got out. Going to follow constitutional channels are you? (*He laughs*)

CIARAN: I'll tell you what: forget the drink. And fuck off, will ye?

KEVIN: Hey, hey. It was only a joke, Ciaran. For fuck's sake, take it easy, mate. What's the problem?

CIARAN: No problem. No problem at all, Kevin.

KEVIN: Pretty rough inside was it? Having difficulty in adapting? Still, not to worry. It all takes time. I mean, what can you expect after all that length of time?

CIARAN: Nothing, Kevin. I don't expect anything. Not now. And yes, it was rough inside but it was also fuckin' marvellous. Fuckin' wonderful. Words couldn't describe it. But then you wouldn't understand . . .

KEVIN: No. But each man to his calling. Some of us did have work to do on the outside as well. And we've had to adapt to some very tricky situations too. There's no blueprint for this little number, you know; I mean, it's not just the Brits we're fighting. We've had the Vatican legions here as well, you know — Ringo the smiling Pole or John Paul II to the faithful.

CIARAN: Aye, I heard. In fact I've heard about nothing else since I got out. Even my fuckin' father seems to have been taken in by the Roman charade! He was even trying to explain to me why the great successor of St Peter couldn't venture North . . . bloody Drogheda!

KEVIN: Well, there you have it. And they all flocked down from here to go and see him. And then there was the youngsters all going to Galway to 'sing for peace'.

CIARAN: Oh, I know there's great hope in the youth of Ireland. Whatever happened to the days when the Bishop came to visit the Falls — 'Take the barricades down,' he said and was told to 'FUCK OFF' back to his Palace on the Antrim Road.

KEVIN: Like, I was saying. Us on the outside have had some tricky things to deal with — playing politics with the enemy within is much more difficult than dealing with the boys in khaki.

CIARAN: What's wrong with people, Kevin? How many more times do they have to be shat on by the Church and its ministers before they waken up to recognize them as a more insidious enemy than any Brit swinging an S.L.R.?

KEVIN: Christ, now you're asking me! If I knew the answer to that one there wouldn't be a problem. Not only would there not be a problem now, but the whole of Irish history would be different, as you well know.

CIARAN: You know, when I said it was fuckin' marvellous in the Kesh I wasn't fuckin' joking. It was. I felt freer in there, behind barbed wire fences, than I do out here, walking the streets I ran about as a child. For all I can see outside is imprisonment, great big fuckin' churches of imprisonment and people rushing like lemmings to prostrate themselves in the name of that captivity. And you wanna know something, Kevin, the whole of fuckin' Ireland is like that. I mean, if it's like that here in the North, just think what it must be in the South. Jesus. I said it before and I'll say it again: 'IRELAND will never be free until there's a priest hanging from every telegraph pole from Donegal to Cork.'

Enter Soldier.

SOLDIER: Fine words to come from an Irishman, Paddy. But I'll have you know I'm a Catholic and a practising one at that.

And if you ask me, like, it's not the priests they want to be hanging in Donegal or Cork but mad bastards like you, Paddy.

Pause

Move it. You fuckin' Irish bastards. Move it.

As they exit Soldier crosses himself. Eyes audience. Smiles. Spot on Priest in pulpit. Priest and soldier exchange looks. Soldier smiles. Exit. Blackout.

SCENE 16

We see Robert. He is dressed in full riot gear. The time is now.

Silence.

He aggressively eyes audience for a time.

ROBERT: (*Calmly ironic*) You've read about it, eh? In newspapers. Books. Seen it all on T.V.? Films. Documentaries. You might even have been there. Once. For a few days. On a fact-finding mission. (*Accusingly*) But I'm telling you now. YOU have no fuckin' idea what it's like. NONE!

Pause

Only a squaddie KNOWS what it's like. What it's REALLY like to be in Belfast. He'll tell you alright. He'll tell you what it's like to lie, crouched and cramped, up against the side of a derelict building overlooking a patch of waste ground full of slates and stones, broken bottles, coke cans, burnt-out cars. Pieces of wood that form themselves into shapes of crosses. Rows and rows of them. And with your name on every one of them. Your mate behind you steps on a piece of glass. The noise multiplies. Booms and echoes all round this waste land. And you KNOW there are eyes watching you. (*Pause*) Irish eyes. Smiling maliciously at you, as you squirm and shiver. And dash from this corner to ANOTHER corner of ANOTHER derelict building. And you know that amongst those eyes radiating hate, there is one pair which is cool, sharply focused, and gently squeezing a rifle trigger with a bullet. . .

Sound of gunfire.

(*In a cold sweat*) For me? For me? No! Not this time. Shivering. Shaking. Alert. Terrified. (*Realizes*) My mate! Behind me. It was for him. That bullet. Those eyes. They were for him. Oh thank fuck! Oh, Jesus, look at him! His eyes. Open. Staring. Staring at me. (*Screams*) FOR FUCK'S SAKE STOP STARING AT ME!

Pause

Thick red blood flows over the kerbside. Along the gutter and down into the black drain. (*To audience*) Only a squaddie can tell you about Belfast. He can tell you what it's like. He can tell you what it is to be 'off duty' in an army post in Andersonstown. What's it like to sit on the edge of your mate's sweaty, stained camp bed with a mongrel dog on your lap. And a can of beer in your hand. And your mate snoring. Half-lying. Half-sitting. Always on the alert. Just in case. His head resting against a wall of 'Playboy' tits and 'Men Only' Bums.

Pause

And only a squaddie can tell you what it's like to stand at the Security Gates in the city centre watching the 'colleens' . . . the 'colleens' in Belfast! You stand there searching her bag. She's alright. You say . . . 'you alright, love?' (*Pause*) And she looks at you — as if you were a something even the flies wouldn't light on.

Pause

Only a squaddie can tell you all this. And only a squaddie can tell you what it is to feel fear. REAL SHIT-SCARING FEAR! 'Cause they're not frightened of us. Oh, you can beat them, kick them, torture them, shoot them and they'll scream as loud as the next poor bastard in pain. But that just makes it worse. Not for them. But for YOU. It makes the HATE stronger and stronger. (*Pause*) You can't fight hate with tanks.

Pause

That's what decided me. You see, I swore after the second tour of duty that if ever I was sent back again to that fuckin' hell of a place, I was getting out. I didn't care what way, but I was certainly going to fuckin' well clear off. Sharpish! Consequences? You don't think of ANY consequences when you know you're already in Hell. There's only one way to go from that place — out!

Pause

It was this kid who made it all happen, I suppose. The last straw kinda thing. There'd been a march about them prisoners on the blanket. And after the speeches and that, as usual, there was a riot. Youngsters aged about 10 to 16 clodding us with whatever they could lay their hands on. We were under orders to just contain it. Try to force them back into the narrow side streets. Advance slowly. But as we did that, more and more of these kids came piling onto the streets. Coming at us from every direction. (*Smirks*) We weren't making much headway. So the C.O. decided to use the snatch squads — make arrests. Rough them up a bit as we frog-marched them back into the Pig. We started running. Wielding batons left and right. Clubbing anything that moved or got in our way. There's no innocent bystanders on these exercises. (*Almost bemused*) When this kid — he couldn't have been more than 8 years of age — came from nowhere. Storming towards us. It was as if he had picked on ME! (*Builds up*) A brick in one hand. A broken bottle in the other. He came thundering towards me. I thought at any moment he would stop and chuck it. But the little bastard never stopped. He kept coming. AND coming. As if propelled by some magic force. His eyes fixed on some point around the middle of my riot shield. His face expressionless. Blank. Hypnotic.

Pause

(*Hypnotized*) It was fuckin' me who stopped. The kid didn't. I stood there. Rooted to the spot. In a trance. THEN the kid stopped. Took aim and threw the brick. Then the bottle. I could see his eyes. only his eyes. He shouted 'FUCK THE BRITS'. Then he turned. Turned his back — and walked away.

Long pause. Comes out of trance. Then aggressively eyes the audience.

Only a squaddie can tell you what it's like in Belfast! Only a squaddie knows how fuckin' DIFFERENT they are!

Blackout.

17 SCENE

We see Bucksey and Yap as in scene 11.

YAP: So, you were saying Bucksey, about the English thinking God was an Englishman and that's where they get their politics from.

BUCKSEY: Aye. Well, you see, that's why the Devil says they're Imperialists. That's why they've burned, raped, tortured and killed all over the earth for all of their lives. And are still doing, Yap, as you and I know too well.

YAP: We know that, Bucksey. We know that. And anybody from Belfast'll tell you the same.

BUCKSEY: They think they have a mission y'see . . . to make the world ENGLISH!

YAP: The Devil preserve us all from that!

BUCKSEY: Well, you see, Yap, HE DID. Like you said, he's on our side. And it's why he likes us. The Irish! For we won't be made English!

YAP: No bloody fear. Can you imagine how awful it would be to be one of them?

BUCKSEY: And that's where it is, that we, the Irish, get our politics from.

YAP: From where? And where's that, Bucksey?

BUCKSEY: Jesus, Yap. Are you listening to me all?

YAP: I am, Bucksey. I am. But, Christ, that poteen's powerful stuff!

BUCKSEY: From not being made English.

YAP: Eh?

BUCKSEY: Our politics! That's where our politics come from. Fighting. And fighting. And fighting. All our LIVES. Against being made English.

YAP: Forever in rebellion, Bucksey.

BUCKSEY: A rising every 30 years for centuries we've had.

YAP: Never to be English. Never. Ever. Never.

BUCKSEY: And sure who'd want to be, except themselves?

YAP: The Devil bless the mark. For it must be an awful miserable existence.

BUCKSEY: To have no magic! Sure they won't even let their ONE GOD turn His own red wine into His own blood.

YAP: Protestants the lot of them. English Protestants.

BUCKSEY: And they're full of class and snobbery, you know.

YAP: Even with their own.

BUCKSEY: And they all want to look like the Queen.

YAP: Or worse, the Queen Mother. Oh that's the way they are — Up the Empire! And Britannia rules!

BUCKSEY: Whoever heard of an English revolutionary?

YAP: It's a contradiction in terms. It can't be. And that's all there is to it.

BUCKSEY: And the way they spend their time!

YAP: Going to dinner parties.

BUCKSEY: Ha! Ha! The Devil told me about being at one of them one time.

YAP: The Devil was at one of them English dinner parties?

BUCKSEY: He was.

YAP: And what was it like?

BUCKSEY: Fuckin' awful, he said. For they don't know what a good spud is!

YAP: IGNORAMISES! For sure a good spud is a European delicacy.

BUCKSEY: And, he said, they all sat talking at one another and impressing themselves.

YAP: Oh, the English could always talk, but I've yet to meet one that can hold a conversation. And what about the drink? Did he mention the drink?

BUCKSEY: He said it was just like heaven.

YAP: Don't tell me. Nothing but that fuckin' red wine.

BUCKSEY: And none too much of it, by all accounts.

YAP: Ach, sure they're as miserable as virtue itself.

BUCKSEY: And she's mean.

YAP: Oh, my father always said, an Englishman could sit over the ONE pint of beer all night and him talking about the inclement weather and his stocks and shares. 'English culture'. That's what he called it.

BUCKSEY: Aye. And you'd think if they'd no magic, they'd drink to kid themselves on they had.

YAP: NO MAGIC.

BUCKSEY: NO REBELLION.

YAP: NO LIFE.

BUCKSEY: THE DEVIL HELP THEM.

We see Marilyn seated at a table.

MARILYN: Europa Hotel. Great Victoria Street. Belfast. Northern Ireland. 1981.

Pause. Drinks.

To tell 'the truth' is impossible. One can only tell what one sees to be the truth. And the truth about Northern Ireland is the first casualty.

Pause.

I have tried to tell the truth, as I see it, about Northern Ireland. And about Britain's involvement there. For twelve long years I have tried. From CS gas and protest to gelignite and sten. I have borne witness and recorded. Researched and explained. Explained. Explained.

Pause.

But this is the war no-one wants to hear about. Today, a dead British soldier shot, blown to pieces in Northern Ireland, is — if he is lucky — two inches of column on Page 4 of an English newspaper.

Pause.

A dead Irish man or woman disappears without trace. Mourned only by close family. Only if they have the capacity to still mourn.

Pause.

This is one of the longest of the many wars of the 20th century. I have seen it. I have written about it. I have tried to tell the truth about it. My truth!

Pause.

But no one cares. . .

Pause.

. . . no one cares. . .
. . . no one fucking cares!

Pause.

Blackout.

19 SCENE

Final Tableau scene.
We see Marilyn as end of scene 19.

We see Robert as end of scene 16/helmet and rifle. Says the last lines of Only Squaddie speech.

We see Priest as end of scene 17. Final Blessing.

We see Ciaran/in prison/barred lighting.

CIARAN: For our power is that you can't intern our minds. Not in here you can't. In here — is where FREEDOM is.

Music/Blackout.

ACT OF UNION

**A play
in 13 scenes**

ACT OF UNION was first performed as a Rehearsed Reading at the I.C.A. in June 1980. Its first full production was at the Soho Poly Theatre Club, London, in November 1980 and transferred to The Drill Hall Theatre.

CAST

MAISIE/NURSE	Valerie Lilley
SEAN/PRISON WARDER/SOLDIER	Mark Lambert
STAN/PRISONER	Michael McKnight
SIDNEY MILLER/BUCKSEY/A PROTESTANT	
	Declan Mulholland
PADDY/YAP/A CATHOLIC	Patch Connolly

The play was directed by Julia Pascal.

CHARACTERS

MAISIE
SGT. SEAN FITZGERALD
STAN
SIDNEY MILLER
PADDY
BUCKSEY
YAP

PRISONER
PRISON WARDER
CATHOLIC
PROTESTANT
NURSE
SOLDIER

1 SCENE

Sound of explosions, gunfire, sirens, etc.
We see Maisie, a middle-aged working class woman from Belfast.
She speaks to the audience.

MAISIE   See this place . . . Belfast! It would sicken ye! Honest to
God it would. See, living here. It's like one long bloody
purgatory from morning till night. Ye waken up here in the
mornings, look out, see it's all still the same, an' you're still
the same, and you'd give anything to climb back into bed
again and forget that you'd wakened up. Some mornings,
mind ye, after I get him out . . . make the lunch and that
. . . I maybe go back for a couple of hours and get up about
eleven. But then, sure, by the time you get ready and all,
the day's gone and the housework's still staring you in the
face. And there's the shopping of course (*Pause*) Shopping!
(*Pause*) In Belfast! Oh, I must tell yiz about shopping in
Belfast. Youse people have no idea, y'know. Yiz haven't a
clue. If some of you people had to go through, even for a
week, what we have to go through year in year out . . . just
to get the messages, just to get a few odds and ends to keep
body and soul together, yiz'd be up in arms long ago. I'm
telling yiz, no other people in the world would stand for it.
English people stand for the nonsense and inconvenience
we put up with? You must be joking! (*Pause*) Waita tell ye.
Just to give you an idea of what it's like, like. The other day,
a neighbour of mine, Mrs Murray, Rosie you call her. Well,
she'd had her hair done, y'see. Curly. Real tight curls . . .
What's this the young ones call it . . . ? An Afro, is it . . . ?
Something like that. Anyway, off she goes into the town in
a people's taxi. Of course, doesn't the taxi get stopped . . .

TWICE . . . by the army and they all have to get out.
Shopping bags. Searched. Handbags. Searched. 'Can I
look inside your powder puff, madam?' All the usual! Oh
you've no idea! No idea at all! Anyway that wasn't so bad,
she got into the town an' all, paid her fare — 20p it is now on
the people's taxis. Still, it's better than the buses. And
that's another thing. Did yiz know that the bus fares in
Northern Ireland are the most expensive in Europe? Aye,
well I'm telling yiz, there was an article about it the other
day in the paper. Aye and sure the bloody things are never
running half the time anyway. It only takes somebody to
sneeze up the stairs never mind throw a stone and the
Ulster Bus Company have the barricades up at the depot.
(*Mocking*) 'All services are suspended until further notice'.
(*Laughs*) Oh, it's a quare geag alright! It's a bloody
pantomime living here in Belfast! (*Pause*) But what was I
telling yiz? Oh yes, that's right. About Rosie going into the
town. Well, anyway, she'd paid the taxi man and all and
was walking down Castle Street. She was heading for
Marks and Spencer's in Donegall Place and of course to get
there she had to go through the security gates at Queen
Street. (*Pause*) You wanna know what the security gates
are? Well, they have them all round the city centre. Bloody
big iron railings! Corrugated iron, about 12 feet high and
stuck into the ground with more concrete than Wimpys
would use in a year! And what happens, you see, is you get
searched. Aye, that's right. AGAIN! Oh, I can see what
you're thinking. What with all this security, how do they
still manage to plant bombs? That's a quare good question
alright, especially as we Irish are supposed to be brave 'n
thick. Well, I dunno, but it happens. (*Smiles*) Maybe it's
the fairies and little people do it at night. But, as I was
saying, you have to get searched to get through the gates.
Sometimes it's the army. Sometimes it's these ones from
civilian security. There's men and women both do it. They
search your bags and there's a body search. (*She
demonstrates both*) Oh aye, what you have in your bra in
Northern Ireland has to be all your own! Some of them
would sicken you . . . they go a bit far with it, you know
what I mean. Well, Rosie, Mrs Murray, that I was telling
you about, was standing there in the queue at the Gates.

There's always a queue no matter what time you're in town at. Well, she was standing there, anyway, waiting for this hussy to look in her bag and the rest and funny, she said afterwards, that as she was standing waiting, she had an awful feeling she was going to have bother with this one. So, this security woman, like, is looking in Rosie's handbag, going through it with a fine tooth comb, opened up the wee bottle with Rosie's valium tablets in it and everything, and then, having satisfied her curiosity with that, she turns to Rosie to body-search her. And here, Jesus, ye'll never believe what she done. Not only did she feel down her and that but didn't she start poking about in Rosie's new, what d'ye call it? . . . Afro hairdo . . . poking and patting and going on . . . For incendiaries, she says! They'd been instructed, she says. She was only following orders. Says she, it had been observed by the Army G.O.C. and the Chief Constable that more and more women were having this particular kind of hairdo . . . and they thought . . . (*nods*) . . . the incendiaries y'see! Well, you can imagine what Rosie's thoughts to her were! An' Rosie's an awful quiet respectable woman too. She said to me afterwards she was nearly blushing with shame when she thought about some of the things she'd said to that aul' bitch of a Security woman. But it just goes to show you what ordinary people can be driven to. Living here! In Belfast! I mean, have you ever heard the like of it? Pulling and hauling at twenty quids worth of new perm! I'm sure it doesn't happen in Oxford Street too often, I can tell you!

2 SCENE

A seedy, dingy public house in Belfast's dock area. The pub, though Catholic owned, is decorated with Loyalist/Orange paraphernalia:

Union Jack, Ulster flag, picture of Queen, photographs of 12th July parades etc.

We hear the music of an Orange Band coming from upstairs. Loud. Spot on Paddy, the landlord, about sixty years of age. He is washing glasses behind the bar.

Music becomes muted (Orange Band).

Pause.

PADDY: It's coming down you know . . . this pub. Being demolished. Redevelopment, they say. It's all to do with these new ring roads. Jesus! That's all we need in Belfast, like. New bloody ring roads! Christ! Did you ever hear the like of it (*Shakes head*) Anyway, that's the way things are. It's a laugh when you think that it took the Department of Environment to do what the U.V.F. couldn't! Oh they tried — the U.V.F. that is — they came here one night about 2 o'clock in the morning, a squad of them. Petrol, fuse wires, powder, oil drums — the lot. Oh, they had all the gear. Oh, this place would've went up alright if there had been nobody here. Or I'd been here on me own, or with the sons. We might've went up with it.

Either that or they'd a plugged us. But, here, you'll never believe it. Wasn't there a few of the R.U.C. boys in. Uniformed and Branch men both. And didn't a couple of them leave at about the time the U.V.F. boys were rigging up the gear. And, didn't one of the Branch men, Sidney, recognize one of them. Well, you never saw an operation end so quickly — they took off faster than the dogs at Dunmore Stadium. I couldn't help but laugh about it afterwards. Though, it wasn't that funny at the time. And the names they shouted back at Sidney as they took off in the car. Called him Fenian lover! Loyalist traitor! Republican! One of them even called him a Communist! Christ, did we have a laugh about that one. (*Pause*) Oh aye, in case you're wondering, I'm a Catholic. Paddy Mulligan's the name. Pleased to meet youse I'm sure. (*Pause*) I see youse are looking at the decor. And thinking what are these pictures doing in a Fenian pub? Well, I tell you, it didn't used to be all that unusual. For you see, round here, round the Docks area in Belfast — York Street and that — 90% of the pubs were owned or run by Catholics. We Taigs always ran a good house, public house that is. Publicans and Bookies! The two trades Catholics excelled themselves at, in this city. Well, y'see for years we weren't allowed to do much else. Still aren't!

Orange Band grows louder. Rhythmic menace of Orange drums. Then fades and becomes muted again.

PADDY: And you see that wee band that's playing up the stairs? Well, they've been practising in that same room two nights a week for the past 15 years, three nights coming up to the Twelfth of July. (*Pause*) I wonder where'll they go when this place comes down. D'ye think maybe the Department of Environment will give them . . . what's this you call it . . . rehearsal space?

Pause.

Music stops. Full lights up. At the bar are Sidney, Sean, and Stan. All members of the R.U.C. Special Branch. Sidney is in his fifties, Sean in his mid-twenties and Stan is about forty.

Pause

SIDNEY: The same again here, Paddy.

PADDY: Right you be, gentlemen. Three bottles and three half 'uns coming up.

STAN: (*Laughs*) And make sure you give us Bushmills this time, Paddy. None of that bloody Scotch rubbish!

SEAN: (*Bantering*) Here Sidney. Is Stan allowed to drink IRISH whiskey? I mean, are you sure it's alright? It doesn't contravene the Special Powers Act or anything, does it? D'ye think maybe he's trying to subvert us respectable members of the Northern Ireland Special Branch by feeding us with the uisce beatha whiskey?

SIDNEY: If he was a half-dacent Prod, never mind a Branch man, he wouldn't be drinking at all!

SEAN: It's not very Presbyterian, now is it? And in a Catholic-owned bar!

SIDNEY: And it being after hours and all. (*Looks at watch*) It's gone one, y'know!

SEAN: (*Shakes head in mock despair*) It's terrible what some men will stoop to for a drink.

SIDNEY: Absolutely disgraceful! I don't know what the R.U.C. is coming to!

SEAN: He's a family man, you know.

SIDNEY: I pity his wife.

SEAN: Got five beautiful children.

SIDNEY: (*Amazed*) Five?

SEAN: Or is it six?

SIDNEY: Jesus! I don't think he's a Protestant at all!

SEAN: You can tell by the eyes, y'know.

SIDNEY: Aye! Sly . . .

SEAN: Fenian . . .

SIDNEY: Papish eyes. No offence to you, like, Paddy.

STAN: Have you two fuckers quite finished?

SEAN: Saints preserve us! Such language!

SIDNEY: You know, Sean, (*whispers confidentially*) I don't think Stan's a CHRISTIAN of any sort.

SEAN: (*Aghast*) You don't mean . . . ?

SIDNEY: I do. (*Pause*) HE'S A PAGAN. Left over from the time before St Patrick.

SEAN: Here, Sidney. Do you think the Chief Constable should be told?

Stan impatiently finishes drink. Makes to go.

STAN: Right! I'll see you two bastards tomorrow.

SEAN: Oh, are you going then, Stan? (*Grins*) Take care. Regards to the wife and six children.

SIDNEY: That's another thing. Drinking and driving. . .

STAN: You know, when you two start, it's like being fucking interrogated in Hollywood Barracks. (*He quickly glances at Paddy, but Paddy is busying himself with glasses. Sidney and Sean look anxiously at Paddy. Then towards Stan.*)

STAN: (*Hurriedly*) I'm away, I'll see yiz.

(*Stan exits*)

SEAN: He's an awful man that. . .

SIDNEY: Who?

SEAN: Stan.

SIDNEY: I've met worse, believe me.

SEAN: No. I mean. I wish he'd be more careful in what he says. Or at least when he says it. I mean, saying that in front of Paddy. . .

SIDNEY: What?

SEAN: About Hollywood Barracks.

SIDNEY: (*Laughs*) Oh Christ, that's a good one. Do you think Paddy doesn't know what goes on in Hollywood Barracks? For fuck's sake man, is there ANYBODY doesn't know what we do in there? I mean, they write paperbacks about it nowadays. You know, I'm getting worried about you, Sean — for sometimes you sound like a spokesman for the Army. Or worse, maybe you're a English journalist.

SEAN: That's very funny, Sidney. And you mean to tell me that YOU'RE not worried about people finding out about such things?

SIDNEY: See what I mean — you do talk like one of them.

SEAN: What are you saying?

SIDNEY: 'SUCH THINGS'? What are 'such things'? When what you're really talking about is somebody getting a kicking because they won't talk.

SEAN: Keep your voice down. Paddy's only out the back. He might hear you.

SIDNEY: Look, Sean, I know you're new to the Force but for Christ's sake don't start giving me all that British Army bullshit about 'concern for the image'. This is a war, Sean. It always was. It is now. And it will continue to be so. There's us and there's them. And there's no point in pretending otherwise. That's what your fuckin' army boys will never understand . . . but we do. Least we used to. You must remember, Sean, that for fuckin' years — and I mean years — WE were doing this job on our own. And there wasn't a fuckin' Saracen in sight. And we were making a much better job of it. (*Pause*) I mean, tell me, what does some English officer from Kent who's spent most of his time propping up the bar in the Officer's Mess in Berlin, know about Northern Ireland?

SEAN: Well, they mightn't have known, Sidney, but they're CERTAINLY LEARNING!

SIDNEY: Aye, and who fuckin' taught them? We did. And do you think they say thanks? BOLLOCKS!

Enter Paddy.

PADDY: Well, gentlemen. Can I get youse another? Isn't the wee band in quare tune the night? You know, Sidney, I've always said, that when HE was giving out the popular tunes, HE definitely favoured your side of the house.

They all laugh. Music of Orange Band. Loud.
Freeze Blackout.

The following is on tape.
Between scene 2 and 3

We hear phone ringing. Phone is picked up.

1ST VOICE: Hello. Hollywood Barracks. Can I help you?

2ND VOICE: Hello. This is Mr Raymond Boyle speaking. I'm a solicitor acting on behalf of the Flannagan family. I understand their son, Kevin, Kevin Flannagan, was arrested this afternoon and I'd like to enquire if he's being detained at the barracks there?

1ST VOICE: Sorry, Mr Boyle. Can't help you. There's no one of that name here.

2ND VOICE: Are you sure? Because. . .

1ST VOICE: No. Definitely. No one of that name. Thank you.

We hear phone being replaced.
Pause.

3RD VOICE: (*Flatly*). KEVIN FLANNAGAN. LONG KESH PRISON. 12 YEARS.

3 SCENE

The following scene is to be improvised. Nature of what happens indicated below. Important that everything is carried out with the ruthless efficiency of a ritual. We see the prisoner lying on floor asleep. He is naked but for a single dirty blanket.

Pause

Sound of white noise. Very loud (about 10 seconds)

Prisoner wakens, clasps hands over ears. Sudden cut off of noise. Prisoner is screaming.

A Man (Sean from scene 2) in stocking mask enters, and puts hood over Prisoner's head and begins kicking him.

Prisoner feebly attempts to fend off blows.

Man drags Prisoner up and birls him round and round several times.

Man takes out pistol, places it in Prisoner's hand, then whips it from him, punching him as he does so.

Man inserts bullets in gun, forces Prisoner into 'search position', places gun at Prisoner's neck and fires until pistol chamber empty of all blanks.

Man kicks Prisoner between legs.

Man leaves.

Pause

Sound of white noise. Very loud (about 10 seconds).

Cut.

A Nurse, a British Soldier, a Protestant, and a Catholic, stand at different parts of the stage.

Blackout but for a Spot which moves back and forth from one character to another as they each speak.

NURSE: One a.m. Royal Victoria Hospital. Casualty Wing. Quiet but for one drunk. Six stitches in head. Says he's Moses come to deliver us. DELIVER ME in peace and quiet 'til eight o'clock in the morning.

Pause

SOLDIER: One a.m. Broadway Army Post. Quiet. 100 yards to the left, the Nurses' Home. ONE HUNDRED YARDS! TO HEAVEN! Perfumes. Creams. Silky tights. Satiny nightdresses. Soft-skin. Warmth. (*Pause*) WARMTH!

Pause

PROTESTANT: One a.m. Springfield Road. Quiet. Driving a black taxi. Mate in the back. Crouching on floor. He's carrying a gun. We're out on a job. Two Saracens just passed.

Pause

CATHOLIC: One a.m. Falls Road. Quiet. Just left club. Few drinks. Need a piss. Convent grounds. Nuns in bed. What do nuns wear . . . in bed?

Pause

NURSE: I wish that bloody staff nurse would come and relieve me. She shoulda been here and I'm dying for a smoke. I hope to God nobody rings for a bed pan before she arrives.

Pause

SOLDIER: Cold. It's fuckin' cold tonight (*attempts to strike matches*). Bloody matches are damp! (*Throws matches and cigarette. Pause*) Two cars passed in the last hour. Boring. Belfast can be so fuckin' boring.

Pause

PROTESTANT: Two Taigs in front (*glances back*). Lie low, mate, and be ready. The first one's a woman. Waving us to stop. Don't stop. Go on. The second's a fella. He's looking back.

CATHOLIC: Taxi coming. Shit! There's a woman behind me. Not stopping for her. Must be full. Try him anyway.

Pause

NURSE: Sister says you shouldn't go on nights for longer than six months at a time. Upsets your system, she says. Funny that. I never think of it now. You get used to anything, I suppose.

Pause

SOLDIER: What I really miss when I'm on tour here is — not the booze — Or the women — Sounds daft, I know, but . . . It's . . . it's . . . (*Pause*) ENGLAND. (*Pause*) I AM ENGLISH.

Pause

Spot on both characters.

PROTESTANT: Do you mind if I leave a mate off down Broadway before we go on up the road?

CATHOLIC: No. Not at all. Go ahead. (*Pause*) It's not a bad night.

PROTESTANT: It's cold. But at least it's dry. Do you live far up the road?

CATHOLIC: Glen Road. Just before you come to St Theresa's Chapel.

Return to Single Spot.

Pause

NURSE: Sometimes I think I'd like to get out of this place. Belfast, I mean. Go to Canada. America. Somewhere. Somewhere where there's a bit of excitement and plenty of night life and that. But then again, I got homesick after a month in Manchester.

Pause

SOLDIER: Most people in Belfast are in bed now. Asleep. It's funny to think of all those houses and all those different people in them. All going to bed. Brushing their teeth. Pulling back the covers. All doing the same thing. (*Pause*) Sleeping. (*Pause*) PROTESTANTS AND CATHOLICS. There's a car coming. A taxi. It's going over the ramps.

Pause

PROTESTANT: Slowly. Over the ramps. Then put the boot down. Straight through the lights at the Donegall Road. Right into Glenmachen Street. Left into Tate's Avenue. OUR district. On home ground.

Pause

CATHOLIC: (*Build-up to panic*) What's he going down here for? There's no houses down here. Why's he speeding up? I'll get out here if it's all the same to you, mate. This isn't MY territory. Hand on handle of the door. He'll have to slow up at the lights. JUMP! Make a dive for it. There's somebody in the back. Gun. A Fuckin' Gun. Red. Red Flash.

Lighting effects e.g. spot zig-zags

Hit. Roll. Roll. Roll. Keep Rolling. Headlamps. Coming back. Keep rolling. Roll. Roll. Into river. Wet. Stay under! Stay under! Stay!!

Pause

NURSE: Nothing happening. Nothing. So boring when it's like this. Makes the night very long. Seems like eight o'clock will never come. It's an awful thing to say, I know, but on a night like this, I'd nearly pray for somebody to have an accident. Just to liven things up a bit. God forgive me! Isn't it awful what goes on in a body's mind?

Blackout

5 SCENE

A street corner in Belfast. Outside a Pub, Yap and Bucksey are Belfast 'down & outs' (Winos). Yap is about Sixty, Bucksey is slightly younger.

We see the Yap selling newspapers — the 'Belfast Telegraph'.

YAP: (*Shouts*) Tel-A! Tel-A! Sixth! Sixth Tel-A! Tel-A!

    Man approaches to buy paper and pointedly waits for change. YAP *gives it grudgingly.* MAN *walks away reading paper.*

YAP: (*Mutters*) Miserable aul bastard! Tel-A! Sixth Tel-A! (*louder, after man*) Mean bastard! Sixth! Sixth Tel-A!

    Enter Bucksey, holding bottle of 'BLACK BUSH' in one hand and glass in the other. Drinks, refills glass.

BUCKSEY: Oh! Jesus Christ Almighty! If it's not the Yap. And him selling papers. Times must be bad! Must be VERY BAD for the YAP TO BE SELLING THE Belfast UNIONIST Telegraph. Jesus! And the poor bastard looks foundered! (*shouts to Yap*) What'd you say to a wee half 'un or two?

YAP: (*Without looking at Bucksey*) Away on with ye! And don't be tormentin' a Christian working man. . .

    Pause

    Yap freezes. Frightened and amazed. Drops all the newspapers, closes his eyes, raises his face to heaven and makes the sign of the cross.

YAP: Jesus, Mary and Holy St Joseph! Oh! Sacred Heart, pray for us! (*Drops to his knees*) Oh! Mother of God, save me from madness. Take away these voices. St Jude, pray for me.

Oh, Matt Talbot, show me the way. I SWEAR I'll never touch another drop. . .

Bucksey has poured whiskey into a second glass. Approaches the Yap and puts the glass into his hand

. . . I'll go round now and take the pledge. . .

Yap gulps down the whiskey, opens one eye to look at Bucksey, then the other. Quickly closes them again.

YAP: . . . Christ! I know You suffered for me. Bless me Father, for I have sinned, Oh my God I am heartily sorry for having offended You because Thou art so good. . .

Stops suddenly as Bucksey gives him another whiskey.

Yap gets up off the ground quickly. Looks at Bucksey suspiciously, drinks whiskey and cautiously touches Bucksey's arm.

YAP: (*Angrily*) I'll kill them! I'll kill the bastards! The lyin' alcholic fuckers! I'll murder them!

BUCKSEY: Who? (*Pours another glass for Yap.*)

YAP: Them whorin' reprobates in the hostel! Jesus! You can trust nobody these days. I'LL FUCKIN' MURDER THEM! I'll teach them to try and make a pig's arse of the Yap. Oh, they'll know all about it when I start! (*Starts shadow boxing*) I might be getting on a bit but I can still show them wine-sodden eejits that the Yap can take care of himself. I was good you know. One of the BEST. THE BEST! There wasn't a bantam weight in the whole of the U.K. was a patch on me. Making up stories! Lyin' to me! Gettin' a man upset. And then, when he's just recovered from the news. . . By Christ, I'll fix them 'boyos'. Maybe I won't! Telling me you were (*pause*) DEAD. Blown up they says! Down at the docks! Car bomb they says! Bucksey's away. Gone they says. DEAD! Legion of Mary fella had to go down to identify the body. Dead! Dead? By Christ, there'll be no bodies to identify when the Yap's done with them boys. I'll tell you that for nothing!

Bucksey fills the glass for Yap.

Pause

BUCKSEY: But Yap . . . (*Pause*) They weren't lying to you. They

WERE only telling you the truth. (*Pause*) I AM DEAD. Honest to God, I AM.

YAP: Get away with you. Or I'll start on you. . .

(Shadow Boxes and dances . . . places a playful slap/punch to Bucksey's face)

You're warmer with life than I am myself. (*Puts out glass*) That's a right drop of the quare stuff you have there (*Drinks*).

Pause

BUCKSEY: But Yap. (*Pause*) I only feel warm because of where I've come from.

YAP: Where'd you get that stuff anyway? Had a good day in the Bookies or what?

BUCKSEY: That's you all over Yap. You're selling the bloody papers and you'd never think to look at the FRONT page of the damned thing.

YAP: (*Laughs*). What'd I want to look at the front page for? Sure there's no racing results on the front page.

Bucksey picks up the newspaper.

Pause

BUCKSEY: Here (*As he picks up paper*). Read that headline and tell me what it says.

YAP: 'Belfast's "Bucksey" in Docks explosion.'

Yap looks at the headlines. Shocked and Terrified. Glances towards Bucksey. Light out on Bucksey. Blackout.

The following is on tape.
Between scene 5 and 6

1ST VOICE: Hello. Hollywood Barracks. Can I help you?

2ND VOICE: Hello. This is Mr Raymond Boyle speaking. I'm

speaking on behalf of the Flannagan family. And I understand their son, Kevin, Kevin Flannagan, was arrested this afternoon and I'd like to enquire if he's being detained at the barracks there?

Phone is banged down.

2ND VOICE: Hello . . . Hello. . .

SCENE 6

As in Scene 3 we see Prisoner lying on floor but 'awake'. He stares into distance as if in a trance. A plate of untouched food sits on the floor beside him.

Pause.

Sound of heavy footsteps.
Keys opening metal door.

Enter Prison Warder. He is carrying a fresh plate of food. He removes the stale plate and sets down the fresh plate in front of Prisoner. He steps back.

Pause.

He pushes the fresh plate closer to the Prisoner. He waves his hand in front of Prisoner's eyes. There is no response. Warder steps back. He shakes his head. He walks away. Stops. Looks back. Shakes his head again. Prison Warder exits.

Pause.

Sound of door closing. Keys. Heavy Footsteps.

Paddy's pub as in scene 2.
Sean is sitting at bar drinking and reading newspaper. Paddy is polishing glasses.

Pause.

Paddy is eyeing Sean a little anxiously. Sean folds paper and sets it to the side.

PADDY: (*Hesitant*) Hmm. Sergeant. (*Pause*) You're a Taig, aren't you?

SEAN: With a name like Sean Fitzgerald it's unlikely I'd be anything else. Why do you ask, Paddy?

PADDY: Oh . . . Nothing. I was just wondering.

SEAN: Wondering how I was a Mick and also a Branch man? It's not so unusual, I can assure you. There's quite a few of us 'renegade Fenians' in the Force.

PADDY: Is that a fact?

SEAN: Ninety percent of us practising Catholics. Mass on a Sunday. Confession once a month. There are even some who are daily communicants.

PADDY: (*More to himself*) Strange. Isn't it?

SEAN: Not really. It's a dangerous job. Must be prepared for all eventualities. Always be prepared! Death comes like a thief in the night. Isn't that what they tell you in catechism lessons?

PADDY: Aye. I suppose that's one way of looking at it.

SEAN: In fact, Paddy, I'd say that if you carried out a survey, you'd probably find more DEVOUT Catholics in the R.U.C. than in all the Fenian ghettoes of Northern Ireland. There's a difference between politics and religion, Paddy! (*Pause, grins*) Even in ULSTER. But I thought, Paddy, a man like you would've understood that. (*Nods towards Orange paraphernalia*)

PADDY: Aye. I suppose you're right, Sergeant. I suppose you're right.

Drinks business

Pause

SEAN: How's your son getting on these days, anyhow?

PADDY: Which one?

SEAN: The one that's teaching in England. What's his name? Jim, isn't it?

PADDY: (*Surprised*) You KNOW Jim?

SEAN: I used to go to school with him. St Mary's Irish Christian Brothers, Grammar School! I remember Jim alright. He was a Science man, though. I went in for the Arts. Great man for a game of hurling was Jim.

PADDY: (*Stunned*) Aye, he was that.

Pause

SEAN: Funny the way things turn out. Isn't it, Paddy?

Paddy nods. Turns away to stack glasses.

PADDY: (*Whispers*) Politics . . . And Religion.

Enter Stan. Obviously agitated.

STAN: (*Hurriedly*) Give us a double whiskey, there, Paddy!

SEAN: (*Jokes*) Bushmills of course! You know, Stan, you better be careful or you'll be getting over-fond of that stuff. Sidney's worried about you as it is. Where is the bold Sidney anyhow?

STAN: Not worrying about my drinking habits. You can be sure of that. (*Drinks*) Sidney's worries are over.

(*Indicates another drink*).

SEAN: Eh. . . ?

STAN: (*Aggressive*) You haven't heard? Obviously.

SEAN: Heard what?

STAN: (*Drinks, pause*) Sidney's dead!

SEAN: (*Disbelieving*) Aye! And the revolution's the morrow. They're making 'wee Bernie' Devlin President.

STAN: (*Very angry. Builds to frenzy*) I'm not fucking joking. He's dead alright. Give me another of those, Paddy, will ye. (*Drinks*) Bastards! Single shot through the head. He was getting out o' the back of the jeep in Ardoyne. Died instantly. (*Drinks*) That's four in three weeks that sharp shooter's got. And it has to be the same fuckin' cowboy. (*Drinks*) JUST WAIT! Just wait till we get our hands on the Provie cunt. He'll not be able to Bless himself again, never mind pull a trigger. FUCK ME, is Ardoyne going to get it the night. Every man, woman and child in that Fenian shit-hole is going to PAY for this. (*Drinks*) They'll not fuckin' crow for long over the murder of Sidney Miller! (*Bangs down glass*) Are you right?

Stan and Sean exit. Paddy just stands looking after them.

Lights slowly fade.

8 SCENE

Sound of explosions, gunfire, sirens, etc. We see Maisie as in Scene 1.
Pause

MAISIE: (*To Audience*) Oh, yiz are still here then? It's well for yiz with nothing else to do but sit on your arses and watch the likes of me slaving away here. Some people have all the luck. As my mother, God Rest Her Soul, used to say, the world's ill divide. And she knew that alright! You know that woman, my mother, never had a holiday in her life, sure she didn't know what a holiday was. Reared seven of us she did. And all on her own. My father, God Rest Him, died when I was only two months old. But what was I saying there? (*Pause*) Oh aye, about holidays. Well, waita I tell yiz. Him and me went to Dublin there the other day, just for a few days like, ye know what I mean. It was the first time the two of us had been away anywhere together without the children. They're all up now and doing their own thing, as they call it. Well, I tell you, I was really looking forward to it, honest to God. I'd been to Dublin before, like. Him and me went on our honeymoon to Dublin. And then years ago we used to go on the Enterprise train on an excursion for the day. We used to go even when the 'childer' were small but then it just got too much, what with the expense and the bother and all. Anyway, it'd been years . . . until one night, sitting at the fire, doesn't he say to me about going for a wee trip? So, you see, that's how we came to be in Dublin there, the other week. Well, honest to God, I couldn't believe it! Yon's a place! Dublin! Jesus Christ Almighty! God forgive me for swearing, like, but I couldn't believe it. I still can't get over it. No, honestly, I can't, really! It's certainly not the Dublin I used to know. Oh, I know they used to call it 'dirty Dublin' but it was never like it is now. I mean the dirt years ago had a sort of homely effect about it. It was all part of it, you know what I mean. It might have been dirty and decaying and there were the tenements and slums and that but THAT WAS Dublin, not like it is now. I mean, you NOTICE this new kind of dirt. Us, up here in the North, used to joke about down South. We used to say the grass was greener and that when you crossed over the border you were now breathing God's own fresh air. Well, by Christ, there's no fresh air in O'Connell Street these days! There's nothing but the smell of foreign money! Aye, and talking about money, for that's all they do down there, is talk about money and making money . . . what with their PUNTS and their GREEN POUNDS and their PIGS and the E.E.C. Of course Southerners were always like that. Always out for the money, they were. They might be doing alright now, but the time was, not so long ago, when they would come up here and claim off the Welfare State. You know, when you think about it, you can't blame the Protestants for thinking about them the way they do. Aye, and that's another thing, the price of drink in Dublin is shocking. 84p for a pint of Guinness! And that's where they make the bloody stuff! Oh, him and me found that out the first day we were down there. We went in one afternoon, after having a look round the shops like, pint of Guinness and a brandy and lemonade, £1.84. JESUS! I nearly collapsed with the shock and the bloody aul brandy wasn't even French. It was that aul Spanish stuff. You know, yon stuff that even looks like varnish. And the Guinness was freezing! It was that bad he couldn't finish it and that's a sight in 20 odd years of married life I hadn't witnessed before! But here, waita I tell ye. If all that wasn't bad enough, to crown it all, to add insult to injury, I must tell ye about this wee shop I went into, near Bewley's coffee and tea place. You know on the right there, just as you go up towards Trinity College. It was the day before we came back and I hadn't got anything yet to take back for the kids. Not our ones, like, but Mrs McMahon's next door. Six she has. And sure kids love it if only you bring them back a stick of rock. And I'd noticed in this shop they'd these wee pin-brooches with the Tricolour on them. Ach! They were only cheap but I thought they'd be nice anyway. So in I goes to this shop, to have a look round me and buy what I needed. Well! I'd picked out the brooches and I was handing them over to the woman behind the counter. And I asked her then what prices the rocks were, for there was the standard size and then the big fat ones and I know even he likes one of the big ones, for he has an awful sweet tooth. Well, here, you won't believe it. For as soon as I opened my mouth and yon aul bitch of a Dubliner heard the Northern accent, by Christ, she gave me the filthiest look, walked away and served somebody else! And I knew it was because of the accent! I just knew it was! Well, that did it, for I just exploded. And what I said to her wasn't ordinary . . . about Dubliners, and the 26 counties, and Irish traitors and gombeen men who'd sold us out time and time again. 'Our boys helped to put that flag on the G.P.O. too, you know. Yiz didn't do it all on your own.' Oh Jesus, I told her alright so I did. 'And we're still fighting for it', says I, 'And damned the hand you lot have lifted to help us'. 'But don't worry', says I, 'The day'll come when yiz'll reap your just rewards. We'll fix yiz alright then. Talk to us? You'll be praying on your bended knees for us to talk to ye.' And here, honest to God, I think the aul bitch thought I was going to lap the stick of rock round her neck. And sure I would've done I was that angry and in such a rage, only didn't he hear the commotion from outside, and had to come in and drag me out. I think he thought I'd gone demented! (*Pause*) I suppose when she heard the Northern accent she must've thought I was Protestant. Just goes to show ye how much they know, never mind care. They think of the North and all they can think of is Paisley and Protestants. And sure it would've been all the same even if I was. That's no way to treat anybody. It's not a bit of wonder the Protestants are so frightened of a United Ireland, and, by God, it makes you think that maybe some of the things the Protestants say about the South are right. I wouldn't blame them now at all, after yon experience. DUBLIN? You can keep it! For they're nothing but a parcel of money grubbing hypocrites. I'm telling yiz. . . Paisley's a better Irishman than some of the ones running around down yonder!

Irish jig music

SCENE 9

We see Bucksey and Yap in same place as scene 5. While Bucksey and Yap talk they finish off whiskey.

YAP: (*Excited*) So what did St Peter say to ye when you approached the Pearly Gates?

BUCKSEY: Say to me? Say to me? He never opened his gob! He
just handed me a form and pointed to this desk. I'm telling
you it was just like 'the boroo'. (*Pause*) Only the doormen
and attendants were wearing these plastic wings which they
hit you with if you joined the wrong queue.

YAP: God! It's the same all over. Give these fellas any kind of
uniform and they think they can do what they like with you.
(*Pause*) But here, tell us, what'd it say on this form that St
Peter gave you?

BUCKSEY: Ooooh Jesus! Don't talk to me about that bloody form.
It took me half the cursèd morning to read the damn thing.
It's no wonder there's so few gets into yon place.

YAP: Loads of questions, I suppose?

BUCKSEY: Questions? There's more information asked for on that
form than there is on the Army Computer for the whole of
Northern Ireland. Aye! And that was another thing about it
that pissed me off a bit. On the last page, at the bottom, in
small print, it said that preference would be given to those
who had served in any of Her Majesty's Armed Forces.

YAP: Get away! You're having me on! It never said that, did it?

BUCKSEY: As true as . . . Honest to . . . Anyway, that's what it
said.

YAP: Well, I'll be damned!

BUCKSEY: Oh, you will be! Have no fear of that.

YAP: And so, what else did it say on this form?

BUCKSEY: Oh, it asked for all the usual details. Date of birth in the
world. Maiden name of mother. Details of changes in
employment. Any unusual physical characteristics? How
many times have you had the whooping cough? Had you
ever been arrested? If more than once, your application
was automatically rejected. And finally (*Pause*) you had to
give a detailed account of the circumstances of your own
death and who you thought was responsible for it.

YAP: (*Quizzical*) An' what did you write down for that one,
Bucksey?

        Pause

BUCKSEY: I, very briefly, noted down, that in the course of my profession as a fruit and veg barrow boy, I was blown to smithereens by a car bomb in the area of Belfast Docks (*Pause*) while attempting to procure several crates of apples and oranges which had fallen off the back of a foreign ship. Well, I thought, there's no point in lying to St. Peter. I mean, if he doesn't know about these things, who the fuck does?

YAP: Right, Bucksey! Right! (*Pause*) And who did you say was responsible for the car bomb?

BUCKSEY: I said it was very probably the U.D.A. (*Pause*) Or some other so-called Loyalist paramilitary force who had been out to get me, since, as a young fella, I had played for the immortal Belfast Celtic. . . And I said that if it wasn't any of the Loyalist terrorist gangs then it must have been the S.A.S., acting on instructions from the Chancellor of the Exchequer to get rid of me because I was selling fruit at a cheaper rate than the Common Market agreement allowed. (*Pause*) And — and if it wasn't THEM — and if the British Government and the capitalist press blamed it on the I.R.A., then it was an abhorrent piece of racialist and Imperialist propaganda which the Irish people would not stand for. (*Pause*) . . . OR . . . OR . . . if it REALLY was an I.R.A. bomb then the R.U.C. had deliberately chosen to ignore the warning which had been given in plenty of time . . . OR (*Pause*) IT WAS A MISTAKE! — an' I was one of the inevitable casualities of a war-time situation.

YAP: (*In fits of laughter*) What did the St. Peter fella say when he saw what you had writ?

BUCKSEY: He never flinched. Totally expressionless. There was a long pause. Then he said in a very posh English accent (*Mimics accent*) 'You are Irish. Hmmm! We've been having a lot of applications from your part of the world recently. I'm dreadfully sorry about this, Mr . . . but I do have my instructions! It's out of my hands, so to speak. I hope you understand. It's nothing personal or anything, but we are having to cut back on the number of full benefit claimants, you see. Of course you can always make application for supplementary help. I'll just give you one of these pink forms to fill in. Thank you for your interest anyway. We'll be in touch just as soon as there's a vacancy.'

YAP: Jesus wept! You wouldn't credit it would ye? I'll tell you one thing. It explains a lot about what's goin' on down here. (*Pause*) So, did you fill in the pink form, Bucksey?

BUCKSEY: Dida hell! I told him to wipe his arse with it. Turned on my heel and left. A man can only take so much of that crap. There comes a time when you . . . have to say . . . NO MORE!

YAP: What'd you do then?

BUCKSEY: What'd I do then? I went straight round to see the other fella. Told him what had happened, like.

YAP: What did HE say?

BUCKSEY: He laughed and said that was THEM all over and that I shoulda come round to see HIM in the first place.

YAP: And he let you in?

BUCKSEY: No bother at all. Not so much as a signature was asked for.

         Pause

YAP: Just goes to show you, doesn't it?

         Long Pause . . . during which they eye each other knowingly and then turn towards the audience.

BUCKSEY & YAP: (*Together*) The Divil looks after his own!

         Irish jig music. They dance. Freeze.

         Blackout.

The following is on tape.
Between scene 9 and 10

We hear phone ringing. Picked up.

1ST VOICE: Hello. Hollywood Barracks. Can I help you?

2ND VOICE: This is Mr Raymond Boyle speaking. . . .

1ST VOICE: Listen. Why don't you just fuck off, pal, and forget about it?

(Phone is slammed down)

SCENE 10

As in scene 3 and 6 we see Prisoner lying on floor.

Pause.

PRISONER: (*In trance*) I was in a lighthouse. (*Pause*) A big tall white lighthouse (*Pause*) Lonely. (*Pause*) Lighthouse. They took me to the top of a (*Pause*) cliff. Soldiers. Thousands of soldiers. Everywhere. (*Pause*) They . . . (*as if in reaction to sudden blow.*)

PRISONER: I'm looking! I'm looking! I CAN see it!

   Pause

PRISONER: (*Quiet*) Sea. Calm Sea.

   Pause

   Ocean. Big Ocean. Around (*Pause*) Lighthouse.

   Pause

   Big Waves. Little Waves. Green Waves. Blue waves.

   Pause

PRISONER: (*Agitated. Delivery gets faster*)
   Green. Blue. White. Grey.
   Green. Blue. White . Grey.
   SEA! SEA!
   Green. Blue. White. Grey.
   Green. Blue. White. Grey.
   Green. Blue. White. Grey.

During above Sean enters. Preparation for another interrogation session. As he turns towards prisoner, prisoner screams 'BASTARDS!'

Prisoner pounces on Sean.

Blackout

11 | SCENE

Paddy's pub (as in scenes 2 & 7). Orange music.

Stan is sitting at the counter. Obviously drunk. Gets off stool; staggers in the direction of the 'Gents'.

PADDY: Are you alright there? Mind the steps as you go out the back.

STAN: (*Belligerent*) Of course I'm alright! 'Mind the steps'. I'm alright. There's NOTHING WRONG with me. Just busting for a piss. That's all.

PADDY: Watch how you go! Do you want me to phone a taxi for you?

STAN: Taxi? Taxi? I want no fuckin' taxi. What would I want with a fuckin' taxi? Need a piss. That's all I want. Taxi? FUCK TAXIS!

Stan exits. Paddy smiles and shakes head.

Pause

Enter Sean.

SEAN: On your own Paddy? Give us a bottle of Guinness and I'll have a wee 'un while I'm waiting.

(Drinks business)

PADDY: Your friend is in the bogs. He's a bit. . . (*confidentially*) . . . under the weather.

SEAN: Who? Stan?

PADDY: I asked him if he wanted a taxi but he wasn't having it. What's wrong with the man? He's been like that every night now for weeks.

Stan re-enters . . . sees Sean

Pause

STAN: Would you look what the fuckin' wind's blown in? Sean! The Fenian cop! The Rosary Bead Branch Man!

SEAN: (*Jokes*) What's this I hear, Stan? About you disturbing the peace?

STAN: (*Aggressive*) And why the fuck shouldn't I disturb the peace if I want to? I'm allowed to! This is ULSTER! And I'm a Protestant! It's only Fenians like you (*Sneers*) Sean. . .

SEAN: (*Conciliatory*) Come on and I'll drop you off home. You'll feel better in the morning.

STAN: But I feel fine now. I never felt better. And I don't need any wanking renegade Catholic to take ME home either.

SEAN: Come on now. That's enough, Stan. We'll talk about it again.

Sean takes Stan by the arm tightly.

SEAN: (*Whispers*) For fuck's sake, catch yourself on or you'll land us both in trouble. Remember where you are.

Moves away from Stan . . . normal voice.

SEAN: Are you alright then? Maybe see you the morrow, Paddy. (*Sean winks at Paddy*).

Sean makes to go. Stan eyes him coldly.

Pause.

Stan turns towards the bar.

STAN: Put a double in that glass, Paddy. Like the good Fenian landlord you are.

Paddy looks at Sean who shakes his head.

SEAN: We're away then. All the best!

STAN: Good night — Oice Maith! Sean. Don't forget to say your night prayers!

SEAN: (*Impatient and angry, moves towards Stan*) Well, if you won't come that way . . .

Stan pulls out a revolver. Sean stops dead in his tracks.

STAN: I said (*Pause*) goodnight! (*Pause*) Sergeant Fitzgerald! (*Pause*) And Paddy . . . (*Hands glass to Paddy*).

SEAN: (*Exasperated*) What's wrong with you, Stan? Have you gone stark raving mad? Put that bloody thing away. What the fuck do you think you're playing at?

Pause

Sean takes a step forward.

STAN: NO! (*Pause*) Don't do that Sergeant FITZGERALD. (*Pause*) DON'T BE A FENIAN HERO!

SEAN: (*Firmly*) Give me the gun, Stan. The fun's over.

Sean takes another step forward.

STAN: I said DON'T do it, Sergeant.

Pause.

SEAN: The gun, Stan. Hand over the gun!

Pause.

STAN: You're not a fuckin' S.B. man. Once a Fenian! Always a fuckin' Fenian!

Sean makes to step forward again. Stan fires revolver until chamber empty. He does it coolly and unflinchingly.

Pause.

STAN: Sidney! Sidney!

Slow fade out, fade onto Sidney and Sean in Red Gel.

(Pause).

SIDNEY: BOLLOCKS to them! They haven't a fuckin' clue! If only the fuckin' army and English politicians would let us get on with it. I mean, we have the knowledge. The local knowledge. We KNOW who's who. And we don't need a fuckin' computer to tell us either.

Sidney freeze

Spot on Paddy.

PADDY: (*To Audience*) You know, Sidney had been coming in here for years. Certainly ever since I owned the place. And that's going on for 20 years. Most nights he was in. Never at the same time, mind you. Even before the troubles, he was always careful in that way. It's funny, but before this latest spate of trouble, I never used to think much about Sidney. I mean the fact that he was in the Special Branch and all. It just goes to show you how much things have changed. All that used to be taken for granted. I mean, it didn't matter if you were a Catholic and went to Mass on a Sunday so long as you didn't cause any bother. And the pints of porter always had a good head on them. But it would've been a different matter if instead of that picture of the Queen and that Ulster flag, I'd said I was going to put up the Tricolour and a picture of Patrick Pearse. I can tell you U.V.F. or not, I wouldn't have been the landlord for too long. And the Northern Ireland Office, or whatever it was called then, wouldn't have done a thing about it, even if they'd known. Religious discrimination? It was a way of life. Sure nobody even knew where Belfast was in those days, never mind what went on there. They know a bit more now, right enough. But still nobody gives a damn.

SIDNEY: (*Angrily*) This isn't a war for uniforms and tanks. It's about handshakes and winks and nods and whatever you say, say nothing. And you can't fight it — this kind of war — unless you KNOW the place, the people, the geography, the pubs, the alleyways, the back entries of the Northern Irish mind. And how can a fuckin' Englishman know that? How can he start to know it?

     Pause

PADDY: Still, it wasn't all bad. Even if you did have to keep your mouth shut and say nothing. It was normal then to accept such things. (*Indicates paraphernalia*) But at least the district had a bit of life about it. There was houses and people and pubs. Aye, and wee bands like the one upstairs and young 'uns going to dances in the Orpheus Ballroom. Jesus, when I think back, there was some right characters used to come into this pub. Sidney's father was a real case . . . not a bad footballer — did a bit of boxing in his day too. Used to say he was ashamed to have a son in the police force. They're not worth a damn he'd say.

SIDNEY: 'I never met one I like yet', he said.

Pause

SEAN: Politics and religion, Paddy, politics and religion.
Lights slowly fade out
Blackout.

12 SCENE

A Nurse, a British Soldier, a Protestant and a Catholic, stand at different parts of the stage as in scene 4.

NURSE: Eight a.m. Royal Victoria Hospital. Casualty Wing. Jesus! What a night I've put in. Never had one like it. Hope to God I never have another like it again. Man admitted. Two bullets through the chest. One through the neck.

Pause

SOLDIER: Eight a.m. Broadway Army Post. Geezer found last night opposite Nurse's Home. Pretty badly wounded, like. It's touch and go. I heard the shots, like. It's just down the road.

Pause

PROTESTANT: Eight a.m. Still on home ground. Just heard the news on the radio. Last night's Taig's still alive. Condition serious. But ALIVE! I might have to get offside for a while.

Pause

CATHOLIC: Eight a.m. Royal Victoria Hospital. I'm in some ward. Overheard a doctor tell this nurse that I was lucky to be alive. One of the bullets, he said, went into my shoulder and up through my cheek. I remember the pain. (*Pause*) Never been a patient in hospital before.

Pause

NURSE: Anyway, I'm off now. Thank God! I'm going home to my bed. You know, I'm that tired I think my sleep's passed me. I hope that man's alright. Isn't it awful. (*Pause*) I mean, it coulda been one of your own!

Pause

SOLDIER: Funny, like, but even Belfast looks good in the mornings. It's like that short time of new activity before the day settles. You know what I mean. Milkmen. Workmen with lunch boxes. Early traffic. (*Pause*) I can see the nurses coming and going from the Nurses' Home. Everything's ending, like, and . . . starting, all at once.

Pause

Sudden burst of automatic fire. Soldier stares aghast. Freeze.

Blackout.

SCENE 13

We see Maisie as in previous scenes 1 and 8.

MAISIE: (*To Audience*) Here, it's true y'know. (*Pause*) What I was saying to yiz the last time. (*Pause*). About Paisley! About him being a better Irishman than some of the ones in the 26 counties. In the 'Free State' as we used to call it. That's a laugh! There's nothing 'free' about it! I dunno whether yiz have ever noticed this or not — about Big Ian, as they call him — Paisley I mean — well, you know the way he's always going on about the Loyalists and the Queen and being British and that. Well, have yiz ever noticed the way he says 'ENGLISHMAN'? Ach, yiz probably haven't for yiz wouldn't understand it. But he says 'ENGLISHMAN' the way we Fenians are supposed to say it. You know, with real VENOM, HATRED almost! Sure, anybody from the six counties — Northern Ireland that is — would know by the way he says it, that he doesn't like them either. Mind you, don't get me wrong, for I'm no supporter of Mr Paisley. All that stuff about the Queen and all! But ach, you know, we Taigs and Mr Paisley have more in common than meets the eye but sure youse 'uns wouldn't understand that either. But here, yiz aren't the only ones, for neither would yon ones down in Dublin . . . all they can think of is that he's a Protestant and we're Catholics! But if ye ever listen to him he talks about Ulstermen and being from ULSTER . . . it's the North y'see! It's to do with being 'Northern'! It's different! We're different! Always were. I'm not an educated woman and I haven't read that many books in my life — hadn't time with 5 childer and a husband to look after, but I know enough and picked up enough in the old stories my mother used to tell us as kids, to realize that the North was always different. They don't call it the Fighting North for nothing! And that was long before there was a Protestant about the place at all. (*Pause*) But here, I don't want to confuse yiz altogether, for I know yiz have a hard time trying to understand even the easy bits. You know, if I was one of you people I wouldn't want to be bothered with all this at all. But there yiz are . . . yiz got yourselves involved and yer stuck with it! (*Smiles knowingly*) But never mind, sure, maybe it'll not always be the way it is now . . . eh?

Pause

Anyway, I told yiz about my wee trip to Dublin. Well, I was glad to be back home. Glad to get back to BELFAST. Yiz probably find that surprising too. But there's nothing surprising about it. Honest to God . . . there's nothing annoys me more than when people say 'Oh it must be awful!' 'How can you stand to live there?' 'I'm sure yiz'd love to get out of it!' 'Are you not frightened?' Ach, I know that early on I was saying it would sicken ye sometimes. But I'm not joking now when I tell yiz that I was more frightened standing in Victoria Station in the rush hour one time I was over visiting my sister in Croydon. As true as God, I never saw anything like yon. There was people coming from everywhere and anywhere . . . you'd thought somebody was giving away fivers! And they'd 'a knocked you over as soon as look at you. If you'd a fainted they'd 'a had to scrape you off the pavement! They would! I'm telling you! (*Pause*) Dangerous, Belfast? Here's never like yon! Even when it's REALLY bad. (*Pause, Slower*) I suppose it's what you're used to. What you KNOW. And I know Belfast, like. Well sure, so I should, wasn't I born and reared and lived here all my life? I mean, I'm a Belfast woman through and through! (*Defiant*) I'm part of it. And it's part of me!

Pause

(*Thoughtfully*) You know . . . I'm just thinking . . . that's really what all this is about . . . feeling like that . . . about a PLACE (*Pause*). And you know something, it must go down inside us very deep, for we've been fighting about it for an awful long time. . .

Pause

(*Aggressively*) And I'll tell yiz . . . WE'RE GOING TO GO ON FIGHTING FOR IT!

ENGLISH VOICE: (ON TAPE)   So, that's your solution is it? Fighting. And more fighting. Violence. And more violence. Bloody history repeating itself. Over, and over again.

Spotlight English soldier

MAISIE: (*Shouts back in direction of voice*). Oh, that's choice coming from you, Mr Englishman . . . when YOUR history is one long saga of murder and rape. I mean is there ANYWHERE in the world where yiz haven't left not a trail of blood but bloody lakes of it? And has your friend here been converted to pacifism? Or is the big guy in the uniform just going to a fancy dress ball at Buckingham Palace after the show? (*To Soldier*). Here, son, haven't I seen you on T.V.? You were sitting in a Saracen firing rubber bullets out the back. Was yon' a play you were in or what?

SOLDIER: Missus, I just want to go HOME. I've been shot dead once already.

YAP: (*To Bucksey*). Here, Bucksey, what d'ye think happened to that Special Branch man, Sidney, when he met up with St Peter?

BUCKSEY: Oh, I doubt if he had any bother. For going on those bloody forms, I think St Peter's in the fuckin' Special Branch. In fact, to tell you the truth, Yap, I heard from — (*Whispers confidentially*) yer MAN down below — that when Sidney the S.B. man went up — it was St Peter's day off. And — ah — HE . . . was at the Gate Himself.

YAP: And did HE let him in, Bucksey?

BUCKSEY: Well, not only did HE let him in, but I also heard that on that particular day, HE was letting anybody in, so pissed off was HE at having to stand at the Gates himself. AND HE didn't know where those bloody forms were or anything. Hadn't a pen. Nothing. Talk about embarrassment all round!

YAP: Oh, HE'D a been embarrassed alright. (*Pause*) But y'know, Bucksey . . . I think there's more than St Peter in the Special Branch up there. And that's a fact!

          Pause.

          Spot on Soldier/Slow fade.

          Spot on Prisoner in blanket/Slow fade.

MARY'S MEN

a play
in 2 acts

MARY'S MEN was first produced in June 1984 at the Drill Hall Theatre.

CAST

COD ALEX	Carl Forgione
HUNCHBACK HARRY	Toby Byrne
HOOPS MAGUIRE	Walter McMonagle
SECONDS	Tim Stern
BANKER JOE	Michael McKnight
ANGEL FACE	Mike Dowling
PRIEST	James McAuley

Directed by Julia Pascal.

DESIGN

Setting of play is a Legion of Mary hostel for 'down and outs' on the Falls Road, Belfast. Furniture is basic: old wooden tables and chairs.
Specific extras: Crucifix, picture of Mother of Perpetual Succour, Clock. The rest as indicated.

CHARACTERS

COD ALEX: Late fifties. Ex Music Hall entertainer, now permanent worker at hostel. Lives in.

HUNCHBACK HARRY: Forties. Bookkeeper for Wine Merchant, part-time worker at hostel. Lives out.

HOOPS MAGUIRE: Fifties. One-time professional foot-baller, now barrow-boy. Dresses 'smart': down at heel dandy, trilby hat, white collar.

SECONDS: Fifties. Ex-boxer, now paper-seller and pro-curer of wilting flowers. Small, thin, no teeth. Long coat and cap.

BANKER JOE: Sixty. Ex-bank manager. Big, stout man, wears crombie coat. Man of theatre, reads a lot: Shakespeare and Shelley.

ANGEL FACE: Sixty. Old I.R.A. man (at least that's the story), small, white hair, nickname appropriate.

ACT ONE

ACT TWO

PROLOGUE

Music/sound (Belfast Song).
Lights.

VOICE/NARRATOR: Once upon a time, in the City of Belfast, a man stood at his barrow-stall in Castle Lane selling apples and oranges and last month's grapes. The man was Hoops Maguire.

Spot on Hoops.

HOOPS: Right, ladies. And gentlemen. C'mon athat with you. Step right up here and do yourself and me a favour. Must clear the lot before 5.30. Ten apples for 50p. The same the oranges. And a nice big bunch of ripe juicy grapes thrown in free. A bargain at a quid for the lot. Now, Missus, don't you be looking at me like that. I've seen that look before. And you should be ashamed of yourself and your poor auld husband standing there beside you and him weighed down with the shopping 'begs'. I suppose you've been in every shop in town, Sir. Were you at the Co-op? I used to love the Co-op myself. The old one, you know. But the incendiaries got it! And sure that new one's not a patch on the old. No character at all. There y'ar, Missus. Thanks very much now. Did you buy him a drink yet the day? Ach, go on, sure the two of yiz can nip in for one before yiz go up the road home. He looks like's he's busting for a pint of porter. And you're a wee bit pinched-lookin' yourself. A wee half 'un would put colour in your cheeks. Lovely cheeks, you have,

Missus. Hasn't she got lovely cheeks, Sir? All the best now. Safe home. Mind out now for the bullets and bombs. Right, Gorgeous. What can I get for you now? The same again. Come along now, people of Belfast. Apples and oranges. Fifty pence for ten. Must get rid of them. What's wrong with you then? You're looking awful cross. Would he not come out with you? Is he in the bookies? The pub? Sure, I don't understand why yiz marry us at all! What's that, love? Oh, neither do you! That'll be a pound. Thanks very much now. All the best. Tell him he'll have to change his ways quick or I'll run off with you to a deserted island. Right now, ladies and gentlemen. Only a few left. And they're going cheap, like myself. A pound they were. What do you say? Seventy pence the lot? Seventy pence, ladies and gentlemen. Seventy pence. You'll not get a bargain like it again. Not even in British Homes Stores. Come along now everyone. It's time I was away home. My mammy doesn't know I'm out. Step right up now. Where else can you buy your fruit without being searched three times? Come on, now, quick. It's your last chance. Fifty pence for the lot. Fifty pence! What's that? You'll take the box for £2.50? Make it three quid, Sir, and it's yours. Right you are. Done! Thanks very much now. And a very good night to you. Mind out for the bullets and the bombs!

Spot off Hoops.

VOICE/NARRATOR: Once upon a time, in the City of Belfast, a man stood at the corner of Chapel Lane, selling flowers, freshly cut, a long time ago. The man was Seconds Kelly.

Spot on Seconds. He is drunk and hiccupping.

SECONDS: (*Talking to himself*). I love flowers so I do. (*Hiccup*). I do. I just love them (*Hiccup*). Flowers. All kinds. All colours. All smells. (*Hiccups. Giggles to himself, infectious laugh which makes him laugh more. Staggers. Drops flowers. Then whole business of drunk man picking up flowers. Retrieves flowers*) They . . . (*Hiccup*) they . . . remind me of . . . of women . . . flowers do . . . beautiful . . . (*Sniffs*) . . . sweet . . . soft . . . (*He strokes them and pricks his finger on thorn*). FUCK! (*Drops them again*).

Spot off.

VOICE/NARRATOR: Once upon a time, in the City of Belfast, a man sat on a bench in the Falls Park, reading. The man was Banker Joe.

Spot on Banker Joe.

BANKER JOE: (*Thoughtful*) Day after day after day. Sitting here. On this same wooden bench. Reading. And reading. Watching. Wondering. Little children playing. Lovers walking. Boys. Men. Hurling. Girls. Women. Playing camogie. Old men, bowling. Dogs bounding. And me. Sitting. Reading. Watching. Wondering. At the Black Mountain looking down on us all. Looking down on the Falls park. And looking down at what's over the wall of the park. The Belfast City Cemetery. Headstones. Crosses. Statues. Grass and soil. Flowers and bones. It's getting dark. Time to go. Home? Time.

Spot off.

VOICE/NARRATOR: Once upon a time, in the City of Belfast, a man sat drinking in a back-street club off the Falls Road. The man was Angel Face.

Spot on Angel Face.

ANGEL FACE: Hey, boy! Are you listening to me? So I says to him, this wee get of a Saxon soldier — couldn't have been more than that height — I says to him: 'What do you mean English? What do you mean you want me to give you my name in English? I'm Irish', I says. 'Born and bred Irish from the time of the Flood', I says. 'And my name's Irish. Gaelic', I says. 'And if you don't like it, you can lump it, son.' That's what I said to him. Oh, I told him in no uncertain terms! The size of him . . . that height he was (*indicates, he's got smaller*). And he could have been my son, God and His Mother forbid like, for he looked like he'd just left the elementary school, all spots and pimples, he was. So, what happened? What happened? Well, I'll tell you what happened now in a minute. Is there any chance of another pint here, Squire, before I have to go? Thanks very much. You're a gentleman and a scholar. A true Irishman. Slainte! What? Oh, aye. Well, I says to him then, this wee skitter of a Brit (*indicates size, even smaller*). I says to him: 'And what are you doing so far from home?' Says I. 'Does your mammy know you're out? Have you no home of your own to go to without coming into other people's without so much as an invite?' And, you know, he was that thick and stupid, I don't think he understood a word I was saying. So he says to me, could I repeat that. (*Mock Cockney*) 'What's that, mate?' You know the strange way they have of talking. So, you know what I did (*laughs*) . . . you know what I did? . . . I repeated it for him — in Irish! In the Gaelic. Eh? What the fuck do you mean, I don't speak Irish? What do you think that there is? (*Points to gold fainne in his lapel*) Eh? Eh? Hey boy! Where do you think you're going? Come back here. Come back. You promised me another pint, you Brit-lovin' shitehawk. I'm warning you. I'll have you done. I'll have you fuckin' murdered!

Spot off.

VOICE/NARRATOR: Once upon a time, in the City of Belfast, there were Mary's Men.

Music/sound.

Then into scene 1.

1 ACT

1 SCENE

Lights up.
Dining room of Legion of Mary hostel. We see Cod Alex and Hunchback Harry. Cod Alex is setting tables: aluminium mugs, knives and forks. He is singing as he works. Hunchback Harry is in kitchen, standing by serving hatch smoking cigarette.

> *Long pause.*
> *Sound of front door bell ringing. Harry looks at watch.*

HARRY: Five past six exactly. That'll be Hoops.

ALEX: Who else could it be, Harry? Hasn't he been here every night for the past five years at least, at precisely the same time? Sure don't you set your watch by him?

HARRY: But how does he manage it, Cod Alex? For he's always, but always, right on the spot. It's never a minute either way but right on the button. He has me demented trying to catch him out.

ALEX: Oh, you'd need to get up a lot earlier in the morning, Harry, to catch out the likes of Hoops Maguire.

> *Door bell rings again. Continuously.*

HARRY: Oh, for Jesus' sake, let him in before he accuses us of trying to cheat him about the time again.

ALEX: Alright. Alright. I'm coming. I'm coming.

> *Cod Alex goes down passage to front door.*
> *Opens it — enter Hoops Maguire.*

HOOPS: So what kept you, Alex? Was auld Hunchback features trying to con me again?

Alex frisks Hoops for bottles of alcohol.

ALEX: Now, would Harry do that, Hoops?

HOOPS: He'd maybe try. So what were yiz doing? Saying the long rosary? All fifteen decades of it?

HARRY: Something it wouldn't do yourself any harm to be doing, Hoops.

HOOPS: Ah, maybe. But I'll wait to see if it improves you, Hunchback Harry, and when it does, I'll maybe give it a try.

HARRY: We'll pray for you, Hoops.

HOOPS: Don't waste it, Harry. Look after yourself. Your need is greater than mine.

ALEX: So what culinary delights have you brought tonight for Harry to cook? Bad eggs? Rotten tomatoes? Last year's maggotty bacon or maybe you have a nice piece of prehistoric lamb?

HOOPS: I'll ignore that, Alex. For as you know, as God, or whatever, is your maker, I have never brought stale food into this salubrious establishment. Not for me to suffer for days from the stench of fried onions last seen knocking around Spain at the time of the Inquisition. Besides, I've eaten. I always eat early, as you also know. Old training habits die hard, you know. Dinner for me is at 4.30 p.m. It's what I was used to when I played for the Celtic and I am of the opinion that old routines are the best.

ALEX: You have a quare line in chat, Hoops Maguire, I'll give you that. But here, Harry, have you ever thought that Hoops' chat about training habits and schedules, is — not to put too fine a point on it — a load of bollocks? I mean, do you think, Harry, Hoops, despite his name, ever did play for the green and white hoops of Belfast Celtic?

HARRY: Cod Alex, I can only say that there have been moments when I have been tormented by such dark thoughts of doubt as to the truth and reality of that claim. . .

HOOPS: And yiz'll both be tormented by something else if the two of ye carry on the way you're going. Haven't I the medal and newspaper cuttings to prove it? There wasn't a forward like me. I was brilliant. Oh, you can name all the names you like — Charlie Tully, Jimmy McIlroy, Georgie Best — but there was none of them, none of them, a patch on the mesmerizing skills of Hoops Maguire.

ALEX: Now, isn't that strange, Harry? For it must have been those same mesmerizing skills that kept Hoops in the Celtic second team for all those years. So mesmerizing were they, that they blinded the manager and he, being unable to see, never thought of using such a winger as Hoops in the first team.

HOOPS: That's got nothing to do with it, you twisted bastard.

HARRY: Language, Hoops. Language.

HOOPS: Oh, fuck off the both of yiz! There were reasons for my never being given my due and rightful place in the first team. Political reasons!

HARRY: Oh, political were they, Hoops?

ALEX: Nothing to do with those mesmerizing skills that didn't . . .

HOOPS: You're one to talk, Cod Alex. Star of screen and stage were you? When the only theatre you ever saw the inside of was an operating theatre, with a confused surgeon standing over you wondering why he couldn't find your brain. . .

Door bell rings. Keeps ringing.

HARRY: Seconds out. For that's who that'll be.

Alex feigns boxing Hoops as he passes to open door.

HOOPS: Be careful, Alex, for the bit of a head you still have. Seconds might knock it off.

Hoops then goes into a football commentary — self aggrandizement of himself as player. Addresses this to Harry (disbelieving). Harry pours mug of tea for Hoops. Meanwhile, Alex has opened door. Seconds falls in. He is still clutching several bundles of flowers. And ranting and raving to himself.

SECONDS: The bastard! Bastard! Referee! Referee! Butted me with his head . . . he did . . . butted me . . . ring the bell ring the bell . . . for fuck's sake ring the bell . . . I'm hurt . . . my eyes . . . eyes . . . can't see . . . blood . . . red . . . my blood . . . disqualify him . . . the bastard . . . disqualify the English fucker . . . please . . . please. . .

Alex by this point has managed to get Seconds down the passage way. Seconds falling against the wall, swaying to and fro. He is very drunk and raving. Alex plonks him down on chair. Seconds sits, splayed out.

HOOPS: Good Evening, Seconds. Had a good day? The last favourite won, did it? And it was that last drink for the road that did the damage, was it? Still, you managed to hang on to your flowers. Business is business, eh? You never know, might get a customer at the death. Glad to see you looking so well, Seconds. And you're in quare conversational form. Was that the last fight you were talking about? The one that ruined you? The one that fucked you up for ever — that destroyed your eyesight, your teeth, your nose, the little bit of a brain you had left? Still, you were good, Seconds. You were a bloody good scrapper and you were a hungry fighter, always the best. This town hasn't produced a hungrier or better bantam weight world champion. What a quare pair of hands you had, Seconds! I saw them in action myself many's a time. The number of entertaining Saturday nights at the King's Hall you gave to us all, Seconds, with your bobbin' and weavin' and your right lead. A southpaw of class you were, Seconds: a real champion. And the rebel songs you sang after every fight — victor or vanquished. Oh, what a character you were, Seconds. And what a dab hand with the women, Seconds. Small you might have been but handsome, and when you were in there among those ropes battling for your life and the few bob purse money they allowed you to have, the ladies were cheering and squealing and shouting for you. And when you sang, tears came to their eyes and they loved you, Seconds. They loved you for it. They loved all of you and what you were. All of them — loved you. Beautiful it was. Handsome Seconds and beautiful women. They carried you from the ring with laurels on your head. You were the nearest thing to a Roman Emperor that the city of Belfast ever had. . .

Seconds rolls off chair and onto floor. He has been totally oblivious to everything Hoops has been saying to him, as Hoops knows. Hoops gets up from his table, goes to hatch.

HOOPS: Give us another mug of tea there, Hunchback.

HARRY: Please? And thank you? Go and sit down and I'll bring it out to you.

HOOPS: (*Lifting Seconds' flowers*) And here's a bouquet for you, Cod Alex. Delivered in person by Seconds, the dead hero of the King's Hall boxing ring.

Alex takes flowers from Hoops.

ALEX: We'll get rid of these. Look at the state of them. Who does Seconds think would ever buy these?

HOOPS: Is that all you can say, old Croner? What about the state of Seconds himself?

ALEX: I've seen him worse. What's up with you, Hoops? Getting so morose and sentimental in your old age! Or having joined the Pioneers of late, having been an imbiber of alcoholic refreshments for two thirds of your lifetime, does the sight of a very drunk incapable man disgust you? Self-disgust at the memory of it all, is that it, Hoops? Behaving in the classic traditional manner of a convert?

HOOPS: Would you rather I went back on the booze then?

ALEX: No, Hoops. I wouldn't. But standing there sounding like a moralizing temperance Protestant preacher, I'm not so sure.

HOOPS: You can be a vicious bastard at times, most times, Cod Alex. And you are the one supposed to be giving out charity. You work here, remember, Christian love is supposed to be your business, old Croner. You're the lay priest aren't you: the one who was in the gutter, who now works for those still in the gutter, who knows what's it like? You're supposed to be the one with the inside information, Squire.

ALEX: That's right, Hoops. But it's you that's being vicious. Now, will you stop standing there blatherin' and give me a hand to get Seconds up the stairs? It's bed for him straight away. I don't think he'll be dining with us tonight. Check his pockets there, Harry, for any carnivorous animals.

Harry takes out large brown paper parcel, the stench of which would kill stronger souls.

HARRY: Phew! Jesus. How long do you think this little package has been doing the rounds?

Harry retreats behind hatch holding bag aloft.

ALEX: Right, Hoops. Are you right? Take his legs there. One. Two.

Alex and Hoops lift Seconds. They go down passage towards stairs. There is not a murmur from Seconds apart from the odd sudden exclamation such as: Referee! Blood! Bastard! — after each of which he returns to a completely comatose state. Cod Alex sings song which we still hear faintly as he and Hoops mount stairs out of sight.
Hunchback Harry clears up the remaining debris, flower petals etc., left on floor where Seconds lay slumped.

Pause.

Door bell rings. Three times in quick succession.

HARRY: That'll be Banker Joe. Thank God for small mercies. Sobriety and a little edumacation, as they say.

Harry answers door and frisks Banker Joe.

JOE: Evening Harry.

HARRY: Evening Joe. Turned nasty out then, has it?

JOE: Yes, Harry. It has indeed. It's a dirty aul' night.

Sound of violent thunderstorm and lightning. Joe begins quoting from storm scene in Shakespeare's 'King Lear'. And he continues to 'act' all the way down passageway. (Also, perhaps a section from duologue between Lear and Fool). Harry stands and listens. Pours Joe a mug of tea. When Joe has finished 'act', Harry applauds. Joe drinks tea.

HARRY: Bravo! Bravo! Well done, Joe. You're in quare form the night. You definitely should have been on the stage. With talent like that what in the name of Jesus were you doing working in a bank for all those years?

JOE: Ach, Harry, like many's another talent in this Godforsaken city, the conditions were not present for a blooming to occur. The seed may have taken root and the green leaves may have appeared, but the plant always died or was stunted before the flowering season. Nor was I unusual in that, for Harry, you have no idea, no idea at all, what an immense wealth of talent there has been, was and is in this city of the Lagan.

HARRY: I don't deny it, Joe. There's any amount of actors about alright.

JOE: And not just actors, Harry. Not just real men and women of the stage that wasn't there, but writers and painters and poets and singers and musicians. And sportsmen and sportswomen — for they are artists too, Harry. Oh, when people look and think of Ireland, Harry, and of its artists and artistes, they think only of Dublin and the Southern part of this land, but we in the North have had, and have, more than our fair quota of 'talent' too, you know. Actors like Liz Begley, Joe Tomelty, Harold Goldblatt, J.G. Devlin — painters like William Conor, George Dillon — writers like Sheils, Sam Thompson, Tomelty again, St John Ervine — boxers like Rinty Monaghan, Johnny Caldwell, Freddie Gilroy — footballers like Charlie Tully, the list is endless, and all of them artists, Harry. This city of Belfast is not only the drab, Victorian and industrial slum that some might see it as, and how some of its artists have painted it, I'm sorry to say. But they have normally been renegade exiles, traitors to the mother who gave them suck, fanciful boys and girls who took their given talent from the soil of Beal Feirsde and sold it in the cosmopolitan market places of London, Paris and New York. There have been those alright, Harry, but there have also been those who stayed and did bloom and I'm sorry to say it again, those who stayed and were not allowed to raise their buds to the sun.

HARRY: Oh, I know what you mean, Joe. If there's an argument discussion or fight, it's the City of Belfast always loses out. For we're castigated every way — politics, religion — and now you tell me in the arts as well. We must be amongst the most hopelessly despised people of the earth. It would nearly make you think that the Jewish people have had it easy by comparison.

JOE: Comparisons of who suffered the most don't matter, Harry. But what artists the Jews have produced! Through suffering and pain, Harry.

HARRY: But is it worth it, Joe? Is all the pain and suffering worth it, so many to suffer so that one, maybe a few, can write or paint out of it?

JOE: A question for God that, I think, Harry, not for Banker Joe. Let us just be grateful that the one — the few — have produced it at all. It doesn't justify the suffering, but it may make it easier for the rest of us to bear the world. It gives us hope, Harry, beauty and a reassurance that all is not lost or bad or evil.

HARRY: You're probably right, Joe. That is maybe the way we must think of it.

JOE: I think I am, Harry. For there is another side to the coin. The suffering and pain of the waste of those others who could have given us even more hope, more beauty, and were prevented from doing so.

HARRY: What do you mean, Joe? What are you thinking? Who are you talking about?

JOE: I'm talking, Harry, of those who are artists, those who had talent — those who, as I mentioned earlier, were not allowed to flower, and hence prevented from using their gifts to bestow gifts on us.

HARRY: You're thinking of someone in particular, Joe. Someone special — yourself maybe, Joe?

JOE: No. Not myself, Harry. For my talent, if such it was, was but a small measure against the fountain which sprang from the soul of the man I have in mind.

HARRY: Who was it, Joe?

JOE: Ach, it's a story and a half, Harry. Are you sure you want to hear it?

HARRY: Well, you can't stop now, Joe, having gone so far. Go on, tell me.

JOE: Well, fill up that mug for me and settle yourself and lend me your ears . . . for if it's not a story, then stories haven't been invented.

HARRY: Go on, Joe. Go on.

JOE: It's about a cousin of mine. . .

HARRY: You had a cousin an artist, Joe?

JOE: Oh, he was more than an artist, Harry. The man was a genius. For he had talent in all the arts. He was an actor primarily, I suppose. But he was also a very gifted painter. I remember there were two water colours hanging in our front room at home. One was of the Antrim Coast road and you could feel the granite and taste the sea just looking at it. The other was of Gleneavy Falls — with the water tumbling down over the rocks and them looking like they were enjoying the bathe. And the trees hanging over the Falls as if protecting the little lone fisherman whom you didn't notice at first glance and then he seemed to stand out like he was specially focussed on. I used to wonder if it was my cousin for I believe he liked fishing. The solitariness of it. The stillness. The peace. The boredom. And the violence on the occasion of a catch. With the rod bending and bending and the wee fish fighting for its life for all its worth. It wasn't just a pretty picture of an Irish landscape. You know, Harry, I live with those two pictures in my head and the comfort and pleasure they give me and have given me as I sit and stare wherever I might be and it's them I'm seeing. And then there was his voice. Jesus, what a singer he was and what a range! He could sing everything and anything . . . opera to comeallyou's . . . many's a funeral he enlivened, for he'd nearly have the corpse joining in and it laid out waiting to greet its maker. It was on such occasions only that I used to see him — funerals and weddings. God, Harry, we Irish are supposed to be a very homely, friendly and welcoming people, but the friends one loses through neglect or the fact that it takes one of the circle to drop dead before contact is renewed — it makes you think about our so-called Irish hospitality.

HARRY: We're no different in that way, Joe. We can be just as callous and neglectful as any other people who haven't our 'warm' reputation. But here, tell us, did your cousin ever sing at concerts?

JOE: Concerts. Recitals. You name it, he gave it. Do you know what he used to do, Harry? He used to go to the pictures of an afternoon when they were showing the latest or even not so recent Hollywood musicals, and he'd sit through both showings, for he seemed to have an arrangement with one of the usherettes at the Duncairn picture house — he was a handsome young man with a charm that made women love him — and when he'd come out from having watched the film through two times, he would know every song in the show word perfect. The repertoire of the man was incredible!

HARRY: He sounds a great character altogether, Joe, as well as having so much talent.

JOE: He was that, Harry. And never a bad word to say about anybody. A true Christian if ever there was such a thing; though he was no puritan for he liked his bottle and half 'un as well as any other man. But what I particularly was going to tell you was this, Harry.

HARRY: Yes, Joe. Go on.

JOE: It's a memory of an experience that lives with me even more, I think, than the two pictures. He was in a play one time, years ago, by a Belfast writer called Thomas Carnford, I think. I'm not sure what the title of the play was but it was about the United Irishmen and what nasty things Lord Castlereagh did to them and the Irish people. And it was my cousin who played the part of Castlereagh. Now, I don't remember too much about the play itself — it was on in St. Mary's Hall in Bank Street — but what stands out in my mind is an image of what happened either at the beginning or end of the show. I can see the dark ruby red curtain and as if cut into it were the heads of the actors and a voice naming the actor and the character each played. And the last to be announced was my cousin, OLIVER DOYLE, as Lord Castlereagh, his head appearing in the centre of the curtain. Dark wavy hair. Pencil-slim moustache. And a face of such aristocratic beauty that it made you hold your breath. And I remember him saying afterwards that for an actor to play an evil person was the greatest gift to be given. For it made you realize that no matter how bad — evil — your character was, no matter what appalling unjust actions he had carried out, you knew with your whole soul that this 'evil' man was a man . . . a human being and could never really be considered truly evil. Could never be the embodiment of pure evil for he was also a man, and his humanity asserted itself if only to himself privately. That image of my cousin and those thoughts of his have stayed with me, inextricably linked, Harry, for it has always seemed to me that it holds everything I have ever felt or thought about art and men.

HARRY: An actor/philosopher he was, Joe.

JOE: All of them together, Harry. But quintessentially an artist. In the true sense.

Pause.

HARRY: And can I ask, Joe, whatever happened to him? Did he keep painting and acting and singing?

Long pause.

JOE: He could sing until the day he died . . . and he painted the odd picture. But he gave up what he was great at, and what he wanted to be great at. He stopped acting when he married. The business of life took over. The business of being a 'good' husband and father prevented him from going any further. The business of being a provider for his family. The theatre profession is not a good provider, Harry . . . for a few maybe, but not for a Belfast man born in 1920 with a beautiful wife to look after and subsequently four children. The threatre is not a life for a young beautiful country girl to easily understand or to realize that it is the life blood of her immensely talented new young husband. Perhaps he should have perfected the art rather than the life and not got married, perhaps his wife should have helped and encouraged more than she did, perhaps, if external circumstances had've been different, perhaps, if this city had better known what one of its sons was and had in him to be . . . perhaps . . . perhaps . . . perhaps Harry. So you can see the tragedy and pain and suffering of waste too, Harry. Sacrifice can make art, Harry, but what of those who were forced to 'sacrifice' their talent? What of them, Harry? What of them? And this poor bitch of a city is full of them, Harry. This Legion of Mary hostel is full of them.

Towards the end of this speech Hoops Maguire has appeared and has been standing by door to passage listening.

HOOPS: Your arse in parsley, Banker Joe. This City and this Legion of Mary hostel is full of nothing of the kind. Jesus, I haven't heard so much self-pitying romantic drivel in a long lot of years. You wanna know what this city and hostel is full of? I'll tell you what . . . lice and bugs and cockroaches and it's the people I'm talking about, not the animal life . . . though we have those too, of course. This hostel is full of has-beens, Banker Joe. Fuckin' has-beens and a large selection of never-was's who'd like to think they'd been 'has-beens'. And nearly convince themselves of their case when they've imbibed enough alcoholic liquor to give them the courage to spout and play-act the part. That's what this hostel is full of — drunkards, winos, gobshites, who don't know who or what they are from one day to the next and are hoping that death and peace will come sooner rather than later. For it's oblivion they seek — beautiful drunken oblivion. The high of not being is the desire of those who reside here. And you and I, Banker Joe, in our practised and hard-tried sobriety, are no fuckin' different from the rest of them. So don't come here with your crappy bullshit about sacrifice and talent: the only I.D. needed here is for your passport to have printed on it . . . SHITEHAWK, TURD OF THE WORLD or just simply in big capital letters PLAY-ACTING FAILURE! 'My cousin, the true artist . . . !'

JOE: Don't you dare say a word about my cousin.

HOOPS: Has been's and never was's! And your cousin . . .

Banker Joe makes a lunge at Hoops. Scuffle. Harry intervenes to separate them. Door bell rings. We see Cod Alex appear at foot of stairs.

ALEX: What's going on down there? Everything alright, Harry?

Door bell rings several times in quick succession.

HARRY: Everything's fine, Alex. Just fine.

Harry has managed to separate them and pacify Banker Joe who is now sitting reading. Hoops at opposite end of room just sits staring.
Door bell rings again impatiently.

ALEX: Alright! Alright! I'm coming. Jesus, have you no patience? There's no Claridges doormen work here, you know.

Alex opens door and in steps Angel Face looking anxious and as if he's been chased. Cod Alex frisks him.

ALEX: Jesus, Angel Face, what's the matter with you? You're in such a hurry you'd think the Devil himself was on your tail.

ANGEL FACE: It's worse. Close that bloody door quick. They're after me. They're after me again.

ALEX: Who are? What are you on about, Angel Face? For God's sake, get a grip on yourself. What are you talking about?

ANGEL FACE: Phew! I thought sure that Saracen car was going to stop and I, Angel Face, would never be seen again. For they have long memories those guys, you know. Very long memories.

Angel Face and Alex have by now come down passage into 'Dining room'.

ANGEL FACE: Evening comrades. God Bless Ireland and all here!

BANKER JOE AND HARRY (TOGETHER): Dia Duit, Angel Face.

Hoops says nothing but falsely smiles.

ANGEL FACE: Dia is Muire Duit, comrades!

ALEX: But I thought it was the Fifties campaign when you were involved, Angel Face? What would they be wanting you for these days?

HOOPS: What would anybody be wanting him for now or then or any other bloody time? Another bullshiter!

HARRY: That's enough, Hoops. We've heard all we want to hear from you for one evening. Hold your tongue, Hoops.

HOOPS: Aaaah!

ANGEL FACE: Aye. But you never know, Alex. They might catch on. They never forget those fellas. It's the English have long memories, not the Irish, you know — to do with the drink, y'see.

ALEX: But those wee squaddies out there wouldn't have been born when you were in the 'R.A., Angel Face.

HOOPS: He never was in the 'R.A. He's another fuckin' myth-maker.

HARRY: Hoops, if you don't lay off, you're going out. Now, make that an end to it. You can pay down at the St. Vincent de Paul if you don't like the company here.

ALEX: So, how would they recognize you, Angel Face?

ANGEL FACE: It wouldn't stop them knowing — the consciousness of history, race memory, psychic powers, experiences from a previous life. Oh, don't you kid yourself, Alex, they'd know. Clever bastards, the English — always were — if they weren't so bloody clever, we'd have got rid of them years ago, instead of having failed rebellions every thirty years for the last eight hundred.

HOOPS: Now he's talking. Sense, for once.

ANGEL FACE: But we had memories too, in those days. We remembered then as well. And we never forgot either. For many's an R.U.C man or 'B' Special or R.I.C. man or Black & Tan. . .

HOOPS: Christ, he's been through it all, hasn't he? And he doesn't LOOK that old.

ANGEL FACE: . . . was living far, far away in another land, another country, for maybe 30–40 years and him thinking he was safe and comfortable. And maybe not even remembering where Ireland was or what bloody acts he'd committed in the name of the English Crown when he was but a young buck, BUT we always caught up with him.

HOOPS: Like the whippet always after the hare.

ANGEL FACE: We always got our man . . . in those days. There were men in my day — I.R.A. men — whose life's work was to seek out those, whoever they were, wherever they were, and make them pay the retribution they owed to Ireland. That was the I.R.A. to which I belonged. Full, it was, of committed, lonely wanderers who would roam the four corners of the earth to plug an enemy of Ireland. Dedicated men they were. Soldiers of Destiny they were. And we always got our man!

Angel Face begins singing song 'We always get our man' and jigging round.

ANGEL FACE: Come on, Joe. You know the tune.

JOE: I certainly should, Angel Face. I've heard it often enough from yourself (*Joe laughs and joins in*).

ANGEL FACE: Alex? Harry?

They both join in singing/dancing.

ANGEL FACE: Hoops?

HOOPS: Myth-makers, the lot of yiz. Fuckin' myth-makers!

All freeze but for Hoops.
Light change/Spot on Hoops.

HOOPS: See what I mean? Aren't I right? Myth-makers! Fuckin' myth-makers, all of them. And this hostel's full of them. Not just the hostel but the whole of fuckin' Ireland. Always was. Is. And I ask myself, will it ever be any fuckin' different? For we breed them like rabbits, ROMANTICS, and if there's one thing we have a surfeit of in Ireland, it's that particular strain. We could do with mixing it with a strong dose of Anglo-Saxon pragmatism: maybe the blood would reach its equilibrium then. Maybe we should pass a law that would enforce all fertile Irish to marry fertile English! That way we'd maybe get a balance. The Irish would be less bloody romantic and the English would be less dry and boring and bloody reasonable. It would give them, the English, a bit of jizz and fizz. Oh, I'm all for inter-marrying, the more there is the better it would be. Break the tribal minds, that's what we need to be doing — not fighting for the freedom to continue the incest!

Enter Seconds. He's holding his head and moaning.

SECONDS: Where is everybody? Jesus, my head! What happened? Did I win? Did I beat him, the bastard, the dirty bastard. Hit me with his head, you know. But I'll fix him — return bout. Then we'll see. Christ, does my head hurt!

Others unfreeze.
All go into song and dance routine — 'I'll tell my Ma'. Hoops just watches the 'Myth-makers'.
After 'I'll tell my Ma', boxing routine by Seconds and Angel Face. Sound effects of crowd etc./fantasy sequence.

HARRY: Ladies and Gentlemen. The winner on a points decision and the new bantam weight champion of the world is SECONDS KELLY!

Seconds, hands raised high. Acknowledges opponent and cheers of crowd (Angel Face). Seconds holds out hands to quieten crowd. Then he begins singing. . .

SECONDS: Good night and God Bless you all . . . fans.

ANGEL FACE: Well done, Seconds. You were great.

JOE: You've a right auld voice, Seconds, as well as a quare pair of hands.

HARRY: And now, Ladies and Gentlemen. To continue our
entertainment for you this evening, we would like to call
upon Banker Joe, a modest, shy man, but an artist. Joe.

ANGEL FACE: Go on, Joe. Give us one of your recitations.
Emmets last speech from the dock.

SECONDS: Shakespeare, Joe. A section from old Willy. I don't
understand a word of it but it sounds great. Come on now,
Joe. Up you get.

ALEX: The floor's yours, Joe. Whatever you like. Never mind
these two. The choice is yours.

JOE: Alright. Alright. Just a few lines, men.

*Banker Joe takes out a small grubby volume of Shelley's
poetry. He begins reciting, though never refers to book once
he has started. The rest remain completely silent. When Joe
has finished, there is a momentary hush.*

HARRY: Beautiful, Joe. Beautiful. You're a true artist.

They all applaud and Joe bows in a grand theatrical manner.

ANGEL FACE: He was some poet, that Shelley, Joe. Was he Irish?

JOE: No, Angel Face. He wasn't. He was English.

ANGEL FACE: God, Joe, imagine an Englishman being able to
write poetry like that. I never thought they had it in them.

JOE: Oh, they've had great poets, Angel Face. And the benefit of
a sweet melodic language to write in. But he was a great
man, Shelley, for the Irish, you know.

ANGEL FACE: Is that a fact, Joe?

JOE: Indeed, he was. He wrote a pamphlet about Ireland's need
for freedom.

ANGEL FACE: Get away with you. 'Tis a pity then that not more of
the English read him. Is he still alive, Joe?

JOE: (*Laughing*) No, no. Angel Face. Dead and buried a long lot
of years. Born in 1792. Died in 1822 at the tender age of 29.

ANGEL FACE: Why's it always the good ones die young? And him
an Englishman, and for the Irish, and writing poetry like
that.

SECONDS: Are you two going to go on about him all bloody night?
What about another song? An Irish song! We've had
enough of the English poetry, good though it was, and we

have poets of our own. Give us a bit of the Gaelic there, Harry. Those two pins you wear in your lapel. We know one's a Pioneer pin but the other's a fainne. So you're the man to give us a Gaelic song or a bit of a recitation in the Irish.

ANGEL FACE: Yes, Harry. Away you go there. God, I never knew you had the Gaelic. I had it myself . . . in the old days. When I was in the 'R.A., then, we spoke Irish too, you know.

ALEX: Yes, yes, Angel Face. We know. Real true Irishmen then yiz were in those days. But give over now and Harry'll give us an Irish recitation.

JOE: We're waiting, Harry.

HARRY: Right, gentlemen. Right. Yiz have asked for it.

Harry clears throat and, unaccompanied, sings Gaelic song. When he finishes, all applaud. They shout: Mait tu, go ndeirig an botar leat, slan etc. and various other Gaelic phrases that come to mind.

HARRY: And now, Alex, it's your turn. How about a wee bit of a shuffle and song?

JOE: Yes, Alex. You've trod the boards yourself in your time. I remember seeing you donkey's years ago at the Empire.

SECONDS: And at the Alhambra. . .

HARRY: And the Hippodrome. . .

JOE: Here, use my stick, Alex.

ALEX: Thanks Joe. Probably need it these days for walking with and not as a dance prop.

HARRY: Hat, Alex? Right, you're all set. Ladies and Gentlemen, can I have your warm appreciation please for a star of the old time stage and music hall, an artiste who travelled the world and played in many theatres, but always came back to his native city of Belfast. Ladies and Gentlemen, COD ALEX or — as he was better known in those far off days — HOOFER JONES!

Alex does a medley routine of song and dance, old music hall style. Towards end of this a shout is heard from Angel Face.

ANGEL FACE: You're a great hoofer and entertainer, Alex, but it's

still foreign games and foreign culture. Give us an Irish jig
tune there, piano player.

Angel Face gets up and lets out an almighty Ceili Yell.
He begins Irish dancing with Alex. All join in whooping and
dancing. Lights slowly fade.
Finale: All sing chorally 'The Mountains of Mourne'.

ACT 2

SCENE 1

Early next morning.
Lights slowly up to show empty dining-room. Then we see Harry at
hatch setting up enamel mugs. He comes round into dining-room and
places mugs on tables (smell of toast?). Harry is whistling tune from
one of the songs sung the night before.
Pause.
We see Alex appear at foot of stairs at bottom of hallway. As he comes
down to dining-room he is buttoning up shirt and tucking into
trousers.

HARRY: Good morning, Alex.

ALEX: (*Drowsily*) 'Morning, Harry.

HARRY: I have everything under control. Tea made. Toast ready.
So relax. Take it easy.

ALEX: Thanks, Harry. You're a champion.

HARRY: Sit down there and have a cup of tay. You look a bit
knackered this morning, Alex.

ALEX: Knackered's not the word for it, Harry. Exhausted. Simply
exhausted.

HARRY: Yiz went on a bit after I retired then?

ALEX: A bit? You could say that, Harry. God those eejits'll be the death of me yet. But it's me own fault, for once they start on a sing-song and yahoo session they don't know when to stop. And it's obvious they don't need the drink to get them going.

HARRY: They'd probably conk out quicker if they had the drink. But once they start, like you say, they're so busy enjoying it, I think they never think of the drink at all.

ALEX: God, I'd nearly wish in that case, they'd get sozzled. I'd nearly provide them with drink myself just to exhaust them. As it is, they keep going and keep going and it's the likes of me ends up a wreck the next morning.

HARRY: Oh, never worry, Alex. You can have another doze after we get rid of them this morning. Is there any sign of them making a move yet?

ALEX: I gave them all a shout there before I came down. Hoops is up for sure.

HARRY: He would be. But then he retired even earlier than myself. Didn't want to join in at all did he?

ALEX: No. He can be a right awkward customer when the mood's on him can Hoops.

Enter Hoops.

HOOPS: Did I hear my name being used again in a disparaging fashion? Awkward customer, am I? I, Alex? Maybe being awkward in your terms means I haven't much time these days for a lot of false bloody nonsense. Keep the inmates happy, is that the motto, Alex? Encourage them to make fools of themselves and live out their lies, but slap them down if they really seem like getting out of hand?

ALEX: Good morning, Hoops.

HARRY: Now, now, Hoops. Alex was only saying about being sociable once in a while does nobody any harm.

HOOPS: I know what he was ONLY saying and I don't need you to bullshit and try to soft-soap me either.

HARRY: Nobody's doing anything of the sort, Hoops.

HOOPS: No. And they won't. Not you, Hunchback, and not him.

Look at the state of him! If that's what being sociable does for you, I'm glad I'm not.

ALEX: And what does being unsociable do for you, Hoops, except make you into a crabbed, contrary old codger that hasn't a good word to say about anybody, not even about himself.

HOOPS: Fuck you and your 'good words' as you call them, Alex. Untruthful is the tag I'd put on them. What is it about you, Alex, that gets a kick out of patronizing those that know no better?

HARRY: I think you've had your say, Hoops. Now that's enough.

HOOPS: And old faithful Hunchback, always there to chime in and support. And back up the man who knows what it is to be in the gutter and now lives in the hostel for those who are still in the gutter.

HARRY: Ah, but they're not, Hoops, are they? They're not in the gutter; but that's where they would be if there wasn't this hostel and people like Alex to live in and run it.

HOOPS: You know, I can take your type better, Harry. You come and do your works of charity and maybe sleep in a couple of nights with the 'gutter boys' but then you go home to your nice house with your mother. There is a kind of normal hypocrisy about your actions, but with Alex . . . he who should know better . . . he who has been in the gutter . . . he who has decided to be a real Christian . . .

HARRY: And he who has not sinned may cast the first stone. You know, Alex's right, Hoops, you are becoming a crabbed, gurny old codger. But even worse, you're beginning to sound like a self righteous moralizing preacher. What Alex said last night to you when you were going on about Seconds is right. You're the bloody hypocrite, Hoops. Not Alex.

HOOPS: And is it hypocritical to tell the truth? To remark upon what is real? Everything I said about Seconds last night was true. And he, Seconds, knows it. He wouldn't deny it, and if he could stay sober long enough to see how he's patronized and coded by you two hypocritical shitehawks, he'd maybe find enough strength to land his once great right hand on both your jaws. You and your Christian charity . . .

ALEX: Well, Hoops, if that's what you really feel . . .

HOOPS: That's what I really feel, you whited sepulchres. And what were you going to say? If that's what I really feel, I can piss off out of here and not come back? Aye, well, maybe that's just what I'll do. So, you can stuff your hostel up your arses, the both of yiz . . . Legionaries of Mary . . . fuck yiz!

Hoops almost runs up passage. He meets Banker Joe at foot of stairs.

BANKER JOE: Good morning, Hoops. About last night, I'm sorry. . .

HOOPS: Oh, fuck off!

HARRY: HOOPS! HOOPS! Come back.

ALEX: Let him go, Harry. He'll be back. I've seen Hoops in one of his 'reality moods' before. And like all moods it wears off.

Banker Joe has entered dining-room.

JOE: What's happened? What's going on? I just met Hoops at the bottom of the stairs and tried to apologize . . .

ALEX: Never worry, Joe. He's in a foul way this morning. Got out the wrong side, I think.

HARRY: Sit down there, Joe. Tea? Toast? How many slices?

JOE: Three would be nice, Harry. Thank you. Good night last night, Alex. You can still turn on the old razzamatazz.

ALEX: But at what cost, Joe? Look at me. I'm like a dead man this morning. Age . . . has taken its toll and then Hoops starts going on first thing.

JOE: Always the way. When you're least feeling up to it. You used to do the Empire then, Alex?

ALEX: The Empire. The Alhambra. Couple of times the Opera House itself.

JOE: Ah, Jesus, I love it. I love it. Christ, weren't they great days, Alex?

ALEX: They had their moments, Joe. They sure had their moments.

JOE: And what a city this was — in those days. A REAL CITY! Oh, people might have been having hard times and there wasn't much money about, but Jesus, with the little you had you could do something with it. And it WAS A CITY! A CITY! With shops and theatres and cinemas and people queueing up to go to them — and even if they hadn't the money for such entertainment — God! I remember what it was just to walk up and down Royal Avenue and look in the shop windows. It was a Saturday night out just to do that, and maybe a bag of boiled sweets in your pocket and a pretty girl on your arm and the both of yiz talking and talking . . .

ALEX: . . . and sucking away at the boiled sweets. Or maybe the yellow man or the honey comb and the bulls eyes.

JOE: God, you remember that too, Alex! And the lights. The bloody lights! A cold November night and the lights of the city blinking and winking at you . . . what it WAS to be alive, Alex!

ALEX: Oh, you're a quare old sentimental romantic, Joe. Maybe it's our youth that is gone, that you're paying homage to, Joe?

JOE: Aye. Maybe it is, Alex. But it's not just our youth — not just the rosy memories of our past — but our city, Alex. Our city of Belfast, I'm remembering and thinking about and, if you like, paying homage to, for, God, what of it do we have today? Nothing, Alex. Nothing. What used to be a city is today a graveyard.

ALEX: The troubles have taken their toll on it alright, Joe.

JOE: Who's talking about the 'troubles'? Yeh, sure, they haven't helped, but the damage was being done anyway. Redevelopment! Ring roads! You know, Alex, I'm sure if you did a survey, you'd find that more of the city of Belfast has been destroyed by our so-called City Hall developers than all the car bombs and explosions put together. It was they — our civic bureaucrats — who ripped the guts out of this city and left not the bones clean but no skeleton at all.

ALEX: There's been a lot of changes, Joe. Even before the troubles, it was starting. You're right.

JOE: You know, Alex, I can't face to go into the city centre anymore. CITY CENTRE! That's a laugh! Two soldiers, a security woman and a lost mongrel dog, more like.

ALEX: It can be a depressing sight alright, Joe. There's no denying it.

JOE: Depressing? You're bloody right it's depressing. I've seen more life in a morgue. You wanna know the last time I was in OUR city centre. New Year's Eve. Two years ago.

ALEX: That long, Joe?

JOE: And you wanna know who else was in it? NOBODY! BLOODY NOBODY, Alex. There didn't even seem to be the two soldiers. Just the lost mongrel dog and me and I don't know which of the two of us felt the most lost, me or the mongrel for that matter. The rest was a black Belfast darkness and a cold silence that ate into your mind, never mind your bones. And that was New Year's bloody Eve. In Belfast. In our city centre, Alex.

ALEX: It's no wonder you now stick to the Falls Park, Joe. At least there you've the chance of seeing a man and his dog.

JOE: Aye, there I can sit and listen to the birds and the insects and read. Read and hear the voices of the characters in the book in my head. And look up at the Black Mountain and wonder . . . and wonder. . .

         Enter Angel Face from hallway.

ANGEL FACE: . . . and wonder what? Jesus, you're always wondering, Banker Joe. Wondering and quoting books. It'll land you in trouble one of these days — all that wondering and quoting.

JOE: Good morning, Angel Face.

ALEX: Oh, Jesus, don't tell me you're another one to get out the wrong side this morning, Angel Face?

ANGEL FACE: The wrong side of what? Another what? Ha! Ha! You don't look too good yourself this morning, Cod Alex. Now where's Harry? Is there any chance of any breakfast around here this morning? I could do with a good sweet hot cup of tay — I'm parched.

         Harry appears from kitchen with tea and toast. Sets it before Angel Face.

HARRY: Not a condition you'd be used to, Angel Face.

ANGEL FACE: Eh?

HARRY: Parched. I said not a condition . . .

ANGEL FACE   Aye, I heard you, I heard you. And I suppose yiz are all going to gang up on me and go on about my wee weakness.

They all stifle laughter but nod knowingly at each other.

ANGEL FACE: Can a sinner get no peace around here without his comrades going at him and taking the piss?

ALEX: Nobody spoke, Angel Face.

HARRY: Nobody said a word.

Banker Joe gets ready to leave/puts on overcoat.

JOE: Right, comrades, I'll be leaving yiz. I'm off. Thanks for the tea and toast, Harry. Give my compliments to the chef when you see him. It seems to be a bright sunny morning . . . the park will be in fine fettle today if it keeps up. Au revoir, mon cheri.

ANGEL FACE: Aye, all the best, Joe. Don't do too much wondering now, you hear, them books is going to your head.

JOE: Some of us have the intoxication of literature and art while others have . . .

Alex and Harry laugh.

ANGEL FACE: Away on with you and don't be starting on me again.

Joe waves, goes up hallway and exits through front door.

ALEX: Was there any sign of life from Seconds, did you notice, Angel Face?

ANGEL FACE: No. Never saw or heard anything, sir.

ALEX: I better give him another shout, Harry, for he'll be going out on his ear without breakfast if he doesn't get a move on. It's always the bloody same with Seconds. Full when he arrives at night and dead asleep in the mornings when he should be out. I'll go and waken him from his slumbers.

ANGEL FACE: Watch he doesn't land you one — he's probably dreaming of fights and championship titles.

ALEX: Nightmares of defeat more like, if I know Seconds.

ANGEL FACE: Ah, don't you kid yourself, Alex. He was good was Seconds. One of the best. He could land you one yet.

Alex goes down passage and upstairs. During last few

*minutes Angel Face has been stuffing toast into himself and
drinking tea like it was his last supper.*

HARRY: Enjoying that, are you, Angel Face? You're eating there
like it was the last supper.

ANGEL FACE: Aye. Well, you never know the moment now,
Harry, do you? Like a thief in the night — that's what my
mother used to say when she was badgering me to say my
night prayers. And when she'd said that, how could a
ten-year old boy concentrate to pray. I was so shit scared it
was the bog I'd probably spend the night in instead of bed.
Or I'd lie trying to keep awake, terrified that if I should fall
asleep I might never waken up again. She said that to me as
well: 'You might never waken, son, so say your prayers and
prepare your soul, for God has arranged it that death comes
like a thief in the night'. Great Catholic, my mother, you
know, Harry. Wonderful woman. Very pious. Very
religious. She must have had a special arrangement with
God, for the thief didn't come for her until she was 96 and
she'd had plenty of warning (*Drinks last dregs of tea, puts
mug and plate aside*). Now that was grand, Harry.

HARRY: You did seem to enjoy it.

ANGEL FACE: You can give my compliments to the chef along with
Banker Joe's.

HARRY: Thank you, Angel Face. I'll do that.

ANGEL FACE: Nice man — Joe. But he's full of arts and farts
sometimes . . . can get on your nerves.

HARRY: And your nerves are bad, are they, Angel Face?

ANGEL FACE: Well, as a matter of fact they're not too good at the
moment, Harry — which is why I'd like to have a quiet
word with you, Harry, before Alex comes back. Alex
doesn't understand, but you, Harry. . .

HARRY: No, Angel Face. No.

ANGEL FACE: No what? What are you saying no to? I haven't
asked you anything yet. . .

HARRY: But I know only too well what it is, Angel Face. And it's
not on. It's against the rules and that's that. The place can't
be run any other way.

ANGEL FACE: But you don't understand, Harry.

HARRY: I understand very well, Angel Face. And I know what you're after and if Alex knew what you were asking, you might not even get back in for the night, never mind what you're wanting . . .

ANGEL FACE: But Harry, it's not safe for me to walk the streets.

HARRY: It's safer for you than it is for most. Now, don't give me any of that old codology about them being after you, and they remember you and that the Brits are running a top secret campaign to kidnap you for an undisclosed ransom for what the United Irishmen did in 1798 or what you didn't do in the 'Fifties.

ANGEL FACE: Harry, it's a dangerous time for us all. There are none of us safe. And if you could just see your way to letting me stay here inside for the day — letting me lie low in the hostel for the day — I mean it's a great cover. I mean who would think — not even the Brits — that a wanted I.R.A. man would be living in a dossers' hostel? Just for today, Harry. The Movement has promised me a safe house to move to any day now, Harry. Harry, you're an Irishman, you're more than that, I know you are: alright you wear a Pioneer pin, so, you don't drink which some might think makes you less of a Celt, but you also wear a Fainne pin. Now, how many Irishmen wear one of those? Some might wear one but can they also do what the pin stands for? Speak our ancient tongue, the oldest living literature in Western Europe and all that, Harry. CAD E MAR ATA TU? TA ME GO MAIT AGUS AN BFUIL TU FEIN? Now Harry, I know you might be quiet about it, but underneath you're a better Fenian and Republican than most. This is the request of a fellow Fenian, a comrade in arms, Harry. You can't refuse . . .

HARRY: I can.

Enter Alex who has been listening.

ALEX: He can.

Angel Face jumps with fright.

ALEX: And I can. And if I find you trying it on again to get staying in the hostel in the daytime, Angel Face, I personally will hand you over to the Brits.

HARRY: Not that they'd know what to do with you, Angel Face. Though if they thought they had problems up to now they'd soon realize they were nothing against having to cope with the ranting and raving of old comrade Angel Face.

ANGEL FACE: Yiz are hard the both of ye. Hard and traitorous. That's what yiz are.

Seconds appears dishevelled and half dressed.

ALEX: Look at the time it is — gone ten! Yiz are all supposed to be out of here by 9.30. Right c'mon, the both of yiz.

Alex takes Angel Face underneath the arms. Harry likewise with Seconds. Both frogmarched down the passageway.

ANGEL FACE: Traitors! Bloody traitors! I'll report the two of you. I'll have you both done. You'll not get away with this. It's a crime against Ireland, that's what it is. A crime against Ireland. Seconds, for God's sake, do something. Hit them both. What's wrong with you? Jesus, you were always a fuckin' awful boxer.

Angel Face and Seconds are thrust out front door by Alex and Harry. Sounds of door being kicked, bell rung. Alex and Harry come back down hallway towards dining-room. Both are laughing vigorously.
Blackout.

2 SCENE

Lights up.
Scene exactly as it was at beginning of Act 1 with Cod Alex and Hunchback Harry. The only significant difference is that the clock shows the time to be 6.35 p.m.

Pause.
Harry looks at his watch and then at the clock.

HARRY: Well, I've got him this time, Alex. Thirty minutes late as it stands at present. Jesus, he'll be raging.

ALEX: He'll not be pleased, Harry. Caught out in such a way and after all this time of you slegging and bantering him. Oh no, Hoops will be a demented man the night. For God's sake don't go too hard on him with the teasing. He was in bad enough form last night and this morning — Christ, what's he going to be like with you having a go at him about the bloody time!

HARRY: You know, Alex, I don't think I'll even mention it. I'll say nothing to him just to see what the reaction'll be.

ALEX: God, Harry, that might even make him worse. He'll think you're being smug about it.

HARRY: I am smug about it. And that's a fiver he owes me, or rather the poor box, for I made a promise to him, that that's where the money would go if ever I should catch him out. And I have. Jesus, I can't wait to see the expression on his face! It'll be a picture. Come on, Hoops, hurry up now. I've won. Don't be delaying the moment any further.

ALEX: Harry! I don't know which of the two of you is the worse or the most childish. For you're both like kids, getting on the way you do.

          Door bell rings several times in quick succession.

HARRY: Ha! Ha! The moment of my delight. Go on, Alex, let him in. I can't wait for this and I've been waiting a long time.

          Door bell rings again. Impatient.

ALEX: Now remember, Harry. Easy does it. Don't go sleggin' him too hard. We don't want any trouble from him. Remember he was feeling pretty sore this morning.

HARRY: I won't say a word, Alex. Not a word. Now, for Christ's sake, answer the door and put us all out of our misery.

          Door bell rings again. Harry business with cutlery and mugs. Excited. Alex goes up passage to door. Opens it and in steps Seconds. Seconds is sober and very different in appearance and manner from his entry in first act.

ALEX: Oh, it's you, Seconds.

SECONDS: Well, it must be if you say so. Who else do you think I am?

ALEX: (*As he frisks Seconds*). Ah, nobody. It's just . . . we thought . . . oh, never mind. You're looking well and different, Seconds.

SECONDS: Different from what?

ALEX: Different from what you were when you arrived last night. You were in a quare auld state last night, you know, Seconds. Could hardly stand — in fact you couldn't — and rantin' and ravin' about some fight you were.

They have now entered dining-room.

ALEX: It's Seconds, Harry. Relax.

HARRY: (*Disappointed*). So I see. And how are you doing the night, Seconds? Sort that English bastard out who hit you with his head?

SECONDS: Eh? What? What are YOU rantin' about, Harry?

HARRY: Nothin', Seconds. Nothing. It was just it was yourself who was. . . (*Alex gives Harry nod to cool it*) . . . never mind, I'm just slabberin' on here a bit.

ALEX: What's the crack with you, Seconds?

HARRY: Any news?

Harry has poured mug of tea for Seconds and set plate of buttered bread in front of him. Seconds takes sip of the tea. He looks from Alex to Harry and back again.

SECONDS: Yiz haven't heard then?

ALEX: Heard what, Seconds?

HARRY: Big news, Seconds, eh?

Seconds takes another sip from tea.

SECONDS: Aye. Big news.

HARRY: Well, Jesus, tell us, Seconds. Don't be keeping it to yourself.

ALEX: Come on, Seconds, don't hold out on us. What is it?

Seconds again looks from Alex to Harry and back again.

SECONDS: No. Yiz haven't heard, have yiz?

ALEX AND HARRY: Seconds. . .

SECONDS: HOOPS IS DEAD.

ALEX AND HARRY: WHAT?

They both move towards Seconds.

ALEX: Seconds, is this some sort of take-on?

HARRY: Oh, come on, Seconds. Hoops has put you up to this. Where is he? Can't face the music, is that it? Can't look me in the eye because he's late?

SECONDS: Hoops won't be looking anybody in the eye ever again, except maybe his maker.

ALEX: Seconds, are you bullshitin'. . .?

HARRY: Of course, he is, Alex. Hoops has probably hit the bottle again and that's why he's late, or else he's sulking about this morning or else . . .

SECONDS: 'Or else', nothing, Hunchback Harry. And I'm not codin', Alex. Hoops is away . . . for good.

ALEX: Seriously, Seconds?

SECONDS: Of course I'm fuckin' serious, Alex. And so was the car bomb responsible.

HARRY: You mean . . . you mean . . . Hoops is really dead and you're not foolin' or clownin' about, Seconds?

SECONDS: Hoops is as really dead as he'll ever be.

Harry sits.

ALEX: When? What happened? How do you know about it, Seconds?

SECONDS: I was with him, wasn't I? Met him this afternoon down at the market.

Harry has switched on radio, the end of news broadcast. They all listen.

RADIO ANNOUNCER: And here again are the main points of the news: A car bomb went off earlier this afternoon in the markets area of the city, killing one man and injuring several others. The body of the dead man has been identified as one JOHN MAGUIRE, better known as HOOPS, a one time professional footballer and well-known Belfast character. A spokesman for the R.U.C. said that a warning was given ten minutes after the bomb had exploded. The Prime Minister, Mrs. Thatcher, said today that Britain was in danger of becoming a nation of . . .

Harry switches off radio automatically.

Silence.

Alex has also sat down. He looks at Harry and then at Seconds.

SECONDS: Believe me now, you two? Take the word of the B.B.C. for gospel and yiz wouldn't accept what Seconds Kelly has to say.

Pause.

Door bell rings incessantly.

Pause.

HARRY: I'll get it.

Harry gets up looking dazed. Goes down passage to front door.

ALEX: What did you mean you were with him, Seconds?

SECONDS: I mean I was with him. I was in the Black Bull all day with him.

ALEX: Hoops was drinking?

SECONDS: Like it was going out of fashion. But you know Hoops, he could drink for weeks without stopping and he'd still know exactly how many apples and oranges were on the barrow, and what change he'd given to the fat woman he'd served at ten-thirty last Friday morning. He was alright. Perfectly alright. He looked and behaved more soberly than you do now, Alex.

At this point Harry and Angel Face have entered dining-room.

ANGEL FACE: (*Drunk*) What's going on around here? Alex . . . Alex. . . I have a complaint to make about this deformed ninny.

ALEX: Sit down, Angel Face. And be quiet.

ANGEL FACE: Don't you tell Angel Face to sit down and be quiet — for I won't. Who do think you are anyway? You think I don't know yiz are both in league? It's a conspiracy — a bloody conspiracy — that's what it is. Do you know your friend here could've had me lifted he was so bloody long in opening that damn door? And then, when he did, he starts roughin' me up and shouting at me to shut my drunken mouth. Christian charity that is. . . (*Alex looks disturbed and at Harry/exchange of looks*) . . . I'm not drunk anyway. Not drunk. A wee bit tipsy maybe. But I'm not drunk. (*He giggles drunkenly*).

ALEX: I won't tell you again, Angel Face. Sit down and belt up.

ANGEL FACE: No. And fuck you . . . fuck yiz all . . . yiz Brit-lovin' lackeys. . .

HARRY: HOOPS IS DEAD, Angel Face! Now will you . . .

ANGEL FACE: Who? Who's dead? Hoops? Hoops who? I know no Hoops . . .

Angel Face staggers backwards. Trips over chair and collapses onto floor hitting head on table as he falls. Harry springs up to check if Angel Face has seriously hurt himself. He hasn't. Leaves Angel Face sprawled out on floor.

ALEX: Never mind him, Harry. He's alright. He's got bones of rubber and a head of steel. So, what happened, Seconds?

SECONDS: Well, I left him in the Black Bull, told him I'd be back in five minutes — I was nippin' across to the Bookies. I had this big tip, you see, told Hoops, but he wasn't interested.

ALEX: Yes. Yes. Never mind that . . . so what happened?

HARRY: (*More to himself*) Hoops not interested in a bet. . .!

SECONDS: Well, when I came back he was gone. Vanished. Then about ten minutes later there was this almighty fuckin' bang . . .

HARRY: Language, Seconds. . .

Seconds looks at Harry, then at Alex. Alex indicates to Seconds to go on and ignore Harry who is staring into distance anyhow.

SECONDS: . . . and it was close, for the whole bloody pub rocked back and forth. I nearly fell over, and it wasn't the drink. For I was suddenly very, very sober, as if I'd been on the wagon for years — strange feeling to have again — and then, of course, all bloody hell was let loose. People shoutin' and screamin' and runnin' out into the street — this way and that way and sirens going and ambulances and fire-engines and police jeeps screaming up and down . . . and God help you if you were in the way of one of those things the way they were flying about . . . greater danger than the bloody bombs they were . . . and then there was panicky shouts that there was another . . . bomb . . . the mayhem was total . . . nobody knew where to go . . . run to . . . or stay put. I thought I'd remain in the pub . . . in the Black Bull . . . but then the cops and squaddies told us they were evacuating the whole area . . . so out I went and ran . . . round the corner towards May Street. And there in the middle of the road was a body . . . well, part of a body for it had no legs and only one arm, and half of its side ripped out, but the face was alright except for a slight cut on the right cheek. Well, Jesus, it made me reel on my heels for I knew the face . . . it was Hoops . . . I just stopped . . . dead . . . looked at him and then I must confess I ran and I ran like I never wanted to stop and all I could see was his face . . . his face . . . my eyes were closed . . . but his face. My eyes were still shut when I was grabbed by this foot patrol of soldiers, who of course wanted to know why I was running. I spent the next couple of hours in Queen Street police station. Making a statement, as they say. Christ, Alex, you never saw anything like it! Never! And I hope and pray to God you never do — that nobody does. To have been with him. To see him . . . whole . . . and then . . . poor Hoops. HOOPS MAGUIRE.

Seconds is near to weeping. The rest are stunned and silent.

ALEX: Harry, will you look after things here? I'd better go and make arrangements about the . . . body. . .

SECONDS: What's left of it. . .

ALEX: . . . see the priest about the funeral and that. I think we'll maybe try to have a Mass here tonight. Bring the . . . body here and then take it to the Church in the morning. It's not far after all, it's only across the road to St. Peters.

HARRY: Aye. Right, Alex. Whatever you think. Whatever you think's best. I'll hold the fort here.

Door bell rings three times.
Alex puts on jacket. He and Harry go down hallway together.

Angel Face is coming round a bit. He mutters.

ANGEL FACE: Oh, we always get our man . . . get our man. . .

> *Seconds looks at Angel Face very angrily. He hits him with a right cross. Angel Face goes out again.*
> *At front door . . . Harry opens it. Alex goes out. Banker Joe enters.*

ALEX: Evening, Joe. I'll see you later. Bit of bad news. . . Harry'll explain.

> *Alex exits.*

JOE: What is it, Harry? What's happened?

> *Harry still frisks Joe.*

HARRY: Hoops is dead. Blown up by a car bomb down at the markets.

JOE: (*Blesses himself*) Jesus, Mary and Holy St. Joseph.

> *Lights slowly fade.*

SCENE 3

Lights up.
Enter Alex, Harry, Joe and Angel Face carrying coffin. Followed by Priest and Seconds. Coffin is placed. They all take up positions at table facing audience/posed as in Last Supper. Priest lights candles. Pause.

PRIEST: O God, Whose property is ever to have mercy and to spare, we humbly entreat Thee on behalf of the soul of Thy Servant, JOHN 'HOOPS' MAGUIRE, whom Thou hast bidden this day to pass out of this world; that Thou wouldst not deliver him into the hands of the enemy, nor forget him for ever, but command him to be taken up by the Holy Angels, and to be borne to our home in paradise, that as he put his faith and hope in Thee, he may not undergo the pains of hell, but may possess everlasting joys.

ALL: Through Our Lord, Jesus Christ, Amen.

ANGEL FACE: (*From out of his drunken slumber*) I'm not drunk . . .

BANKER JOE: Lesson from the Epistle of Blessed Paul to the Thessalonians (*Pause*). Brethren: We will not have you ignorant concerning those that sleep . . .

Lid of coffin opens and Hoops emerges to stand behind Joe/special lighting effect.

HOOPS: Go on, Joe. Make the most of it. Your big chance for a wee bit of the old theatrics. Clear the old throat there . . .

Banker Joe clears throat.

HOOPS: That's it. The Epistle of Paul to the Thessalonians no less. And who were they, Joe? Some travelling theatre group! Ah, God help you, Joe. Enjoy it. For I know it's not me you're thinking of as you read it, but your own performance in front of this captive audience. Let the big voice ring out there, Joe. Come on, give it all you've got. Makes you feel good, doesn't it? Important. A sense of dramatic solemnity, you might say. Eh, Joe? Playing out the last scene for an actor no longer in the company. Ah, forgive me, Joe, for I'm only geagin' you. And why shouldn't you enjoy the 'live' moment? I can't. I'm sorry, Joe, I went at you about the old arts . . . for there's no two ways about it, you are definitely a bit of an artist yourself. You have a feel and a soul for such things, Joe. But, I suppose, what angered me was you wasting it on these auld eejits surrounding you. But then you'd say, they have a bit of that soul themselves, no matter how tarnished it might be. And maybe you're right too, Joe. For who's to tell? But you wanna know something, Joe? I still think they're a bunch of fuckin' old myth-makers!

BANKER JOE: Eternal rest give unto them, O Lord, and let perpetual light shine upon them. The just man shall be in everlasting remembrance; he shall not fear the evil hearing.

HOOPS: Thanks, Joe.

PRIEST: Continuation of the Holy Gospel according to St. John. (*Pause*) At that time: Martha said to Jesus: Lord, if Thou hadst been here, my brother had not died. But now also I know that whatsoever Thou wilt ask of God, God will give Thee. Jesus saith to her: Thy brother will rise again. Martha saith to Him: I know that he will rise again in the Resurrection at the last day. Jesus said to her: I am the Resurrection and the Life, he that believeth in Me, although he be dead, shall live: and every one who liveth, and believeth in Me, shall never die. Believest thou this? She saith to Him: Yea, Lord, I believe that Thou art the Christ, the Son of the living God, Who art come into this world.

ALL: I believe in one God, the Father Almighty, Maker of Heaven and Earth, and of all things, visible and invisible. . .

Lighting effect.
Spot on Seconds/Hoops behind him.

SECONDS: Hey, Hoops. It's Seconds. Can you hear me? I'm sure you can, you bloody auld renegade . . . wherever you are. Warming your arse by the fire somewhere no doubt. Well, anyway, whether it's hot or cold, sunshine or rain, make sure you're on time for your training, Hoops. You'll make the first team yet. And if you have any bother with some of the lads, just you let me know, do you hear? And they'll have to answer to old bantamweight Seconds. I could still make that weight, you know, Hoops. And you know, Hoops, I was good. You saw me at the King's Hall many's a Saturday night when yiz came over after the game.

Pause.

Jesus, an auld funeral makes you think, Hoops. Not about the dead one but about yourself. About your own death. For that's what I thought when I saw you lying in the street the day. I was running — not from you, but from me own death. . .

HOOPS: Oh, for Christ's sake, stop snivelling, Seconds. If there's one thing I can't stand, it's a whingeing fighter. Besides, cry for yourself, if you must cry. Don't gurn for me. I'm out of it now. No more training ever, Seconds. No more games. No more fights. No more Celtic Park. No more King's Hall. No more myths, Seconds. Nothing. And if it does make you think about your own death, Seconds, don't run. Stop. For you're only going to where you were before you were born.

Pause.
Priest takes up bread. Breaks it.

PRIEST: For This is My Body.

Priest ceremoniously gives to others.

OTHERS: Lord, I am not worthy, that Thou shouldst enter under my roof, say but the word, and my soul shall be healed.

All eat bread.
Priest pours wine from bottle into enamel mug.
Angel Face awakens at sound of pouring.
Priest raises mug.

PRIEST: For This is the Chalice of My Blood, of the New and Eternal Testament, the Mystery of Faith; Which shall be shed for you and for many unto the Remission of Sins.

Priest ceremoniously gives mug to others.
Each take a sip from it except Seconds who continues drinking until Joe removes it from him. Angel Face simply reaches for the wine bottle.

PRIEST: As often as ye do these things, Ye shall do them in remembrance of Me!

Pause.

PRIEST: Be merciful, we beseech Thee, Lord, to the soul of Thy servant — JOHN 'HOOPS' MAGUIRE — for whom we offer to Thee the sacrifice of praise, humbly entreating Thy majesty: that by this service of pious attonement, he may deserve to attain eternal rest.

ALL: Through Our Lord Jesus Christ, Amen.

ANGEL FACE: AMEN!

HOOPS: You're back, Angel Face. How's the old head, myth-maker? Wishing you had a wee half'un to clear it? The cure, Angel Face . . . the cure that cures all ills. No cure, Angel Face. Just postponement, that's all. Delaying tactics, it is. And talking of tactics, Angel Face, what do you think? Me! Taken out by an accident of the Republic, you might say.

But here, tell the lads, the comrades, not to worry. Accidents do happen. I don't blame them for it. A war is a war. And people get hurt. All kinds of people. You must expect casualities after all, Angel Face. You know that. But here, maybe you'd mention to them, the comrades, that a few more casualities on the enemy side wouldn't go amiss. For this place needs fillin' up with more of their sort. Get a few more of their big fellas, Angel Face. Always said it — the only way. The wee ones don't matter — there's millions of them — but get their top men and top women. Then you'll hear screams and get action. It's the way of the world, Angel Face. Always was, always will be. Don't forget now, Angel Face. Pass on the message. God Bless Ireland and all here.

Pause.

PRIEST: Grant, we beseech Thee, almighty God; that the soul of Thy servant — JOHN 'HOOPS' MAGUIRE — who this day has departed out of this world, being purified by this sacrifice, and delivered from his sins, may receive both pardon and everlasting rest.

ALL: Through Our Lord Jesus Christ, Amen.

HOOPS: Well, Harry, you won your bet after all these years. Forgive me for not being there to pay up in person. You'll still put the fiver in the poor box for me, won't you?

Small pause.

HOOPS: And Alex, don't be feeling guilty about this morning. Remember, it was me that went out with anger and hate in my heart, not you. And Alex, Harry — just pray for them . . . the myth-makers . . . and ME!

Hoops returns to coffin.

PRIEST: Go, the Mass is ended.

ALL: Thanks be to God.

They all stand/music — Poulencs 'Salve Regina' — builds in volume. Joe, Harry, Alex, Angel Face carry out the coffin/funeral step. Followed by Priest and Seconds.
Music and lights cut/end of play.

NORTH

**A Play
in 19 scenes**

NORTH was first produced in March 1984 at the Cockpit Theatre, London.

CAST

FATHER CRILLY/LIAM/SAM/ WEE JOHNNY	Michael McKnight
BISHOP/JOE/DEREK SMITH/STEVEN	Mike Dowling
FATHER QUINN/RON/ENGLISH DETECTIVE IRISH SPECIAL BRANCH/ROY	Philip Bird
MRS SMITH/FRANKIE/ELIZABETH	Sarah Martin

Directed by Julia Pascal.

CHARACTERS

THE BISHOP
FATHER CRILLY, PARISH PRIEST
FATHER QUINN, Curate

DEREK SMITH
MRS SMITH, his Mother
SAM
RON, English Building Site Foreman
AN ENGLISH DETECTIVE

WEE JOHNNY

LIAM
JOE
FRANKIE
AN IRISH SPECIAL BRANCH OFFICER

MASKED FEMALE FIGURE

A BRITISH SOLDIER

ELIZABETH, English writer/historian
ROY, M.P.
STEVEN, M.P.

1 SCENE

PROLOGUE

House lights down.
Sound of Bodhran drum beating slowly (played by actor).
Lights up slowly to give half-light/misty effect. Actors promenade round stage area. They are dressed in costume of their 'principal' character.

ACTOR: Once upon a time
there was a land
in the North.

A North land
of slippery clays
and Irish bogs.

A North land
of soft English chalk
and Scottish granite.

A wet, sodden land
whose changing skies and lights
suggested beauty and uncertainty.

A North land
whose cold Atlantic winds
make the skin hard,
hard and separate,
from the soft warm South land.

Separate and protected
by the drumlins
of the Black Pigs Dyke.

Once upon a time
there was a land
in the North.

A North land
of sacred hilltops
druids, seers, Gods
and Goddesses.

A North land
where new peoples came
by the short sea route.

A North land
where pre-Celtic, Celtic and new
all were, become
men and women
of the land of the North.

And they, these people
of the North land,
set up a chant:

ALL TOGETHER: WE WILL STAND OUR GROUND
THOUGH THE EARTH SHOULD SPLIT UNDER US
AND THE SKY ABOVE US!

ACTOR: (*Quietly*)
Once upon a time
there was a land
of the North.

Sound of Bodhran drum — fast loud beats.
Blackout.

SCENE

Lights Up.
Belfast. A Sitting Room in the Catholic Bishop's Residence.
We see Father Crilly, a parish priest in one of the parishes of West
Belfast . . . a Catholic ghetto. He is standing by the window looking
out.

Silence.

Enter the Bishop, a Cork man, aged about 65 years. He is the Bishop
of the Diocese in which Father Crilly's parish exists. Father Crilly is
aged about 50 years.

BISHOP: Good morning, Father Crilly. I'm sorry for keeping you
        waiting.

FATHER CRILLY: Good morning, Your Eminence (*he kisses ring*
        on Bishop's hand). Actually I was just using the time to
        admire the view you have here from the sitting room
        window. You know, it never ceases to amaze me what a
        beautiful location the city of Belfast has . . . surrounded on
        all sides by mountains as it is. I don't suppose there's a spot
        in the city that, if you looked up from it, you wouldn't see a
        hillside or mountain range. And you, from here, have a
        glorious picture of the Cave Hill and I, from the parish,
        have the Black Mountain on the other side of it.

        Bishop who, has joined Father Crilly by window, now
        moves away.

BISHOP: It is beautiful alright. I never imagined the scenery in the
        North could be as awe-inspiring. Sometimes, you know,
        Father Crilly, we in the South think we're the ones with the
        monopoly of fine scenery. But since coming north to take

over the diocese here, I've had to re-think that position. If only all things were as beautiful as the scenery, Father Crilly. Eh?

FATHER CRILLY: Indeed, Your Eminence.

BISHOP: But that is why we are here this morning. It was good of you, Father Crilly, to come over early. I thought it best that we have another little chat before Father Quinn arrived . . . though God knows we've had discussions enough about it. But this latest episode puts things in a somewhat different perspective, wouldn't you agree, Father Crilly?

FATHER CRILLY: Quite, Your Eminence. It does change the circumstances not a little.

BISHOP: What's wrong with the man at all? It's beyond me to understand what he's at.

FATHER CRILLY: I don't know that he himself knows what he's doing, Your Eminence.

BISHOP: Oh, don't under-rate him, Father Crilly. He's bright. And he's been a fine curate.

FATHER CRILLY: Until now at least, Your Eminence. But this latest action of his is beyond me.

BISHOP: Oh well, it quite clearly cannot be tolerated, Father Crilly. We cannot remain silent or avoid taking action in answer to such a challenge.

FATHER CRILLY: His attack in the article is veiled, Your Eminence, but. . .

BISHOP: Yes. But any person with even a modicum of intelligence would read it, veiled or not, as an attack on the ecclesiastical authorities. And those with more than a modicum of intelligence, or for that matter, Father Crilly, those in the Ministry of State, will wonder why we allow it. Internal dissension is one thing . . . but a blazing forthright attack (*picks up newspaper*) on how the Catholic Church or some of its chief ministers as he puts it — I can see the pen pointed at me there — is 'out of step, if not out of sympathy with its flock on the realities of Northern Ireland politics' . . . My God, it makes my blood boil to read it again.

FATHER CRILLY: I can understand your feelings, Your Eminence. And it makes my position within the parish . . . as parish priest . . . more than a little uncomfortable. I could see it in the eyes of some of the congregation this morning as I administered communion during Mass. Their looks were reading me to see . . . 'what do you think of Father Quinn's article in this week's Andersonstown News?'

BISHOP: Does the man not see that even putting pen to paper in such a newspaper is dangerous enough without writing this kind of thing. (*Slaps newspaper*) The barefacedness of it is appalling. Absolutely intolerable!

FATHER CRILLY: A typical column of spiritual advice is what he said it was to be. That's what he told me at the very beginning . . . which is why I gave my consent to do it in the first place. The usual subject matter for such a column in a newspaper is Prayer, Alcoholism, Sins of Impurity — that kind of thing.

NBISHOP: But he decides to use it as a vehicle for expressing his rather peculiar political ideas. It reads like the column of an intellectual Marxist rather than the words of a young Irish priest of the Catholic Church!

FATHER CRILLY: So, what do you propose to do, Your Eminence? What is to be said to him?

BISHOP: Well, we'll see first what he has to say for himself, Father Crilly.

FATHER CRILLY: Forgive me, Your Eminence, but I shudder to think what that will be.

BISHOP: We'll hear him out anyhow. And maybe when he hears that unless he gives an undertaking to discontinue the column, or at least restrict it to more ordinary religious matters, then his right to administer within the parish his proper priestly functions and duties may be withdrawn.

FATHER CRILLY: I see.

BISHOP: Well, we've got to do something to cool the young hothead's heels, Father Crilly. Drastic situations require drastic measures. And maybe then he'll revise his opinion of me as some old out of touch soft-brain from the bogs of the South. County Cork had its fighting men too, you know, Father Crilly!

FATHER CRILLY: Oh I know, Your Eminence. I know.

Enter Father Quinn. (Hold/blackout)

SCENE   3

Lights up. (Shadowy effect).
Belfast I.R.A. 'safe' house.
We see Liam, Joe and Frankie.

FRANKIE: Orders, lads. It's been decided that you two better get offside for a while. Go down below.

JOE: Where? Dublin?

FRANKIE: Aye. That's right. We want you both out of the way for a while.

LIAM: Thanks, Frankie.

FRANKIE: We don't want you getting picked up. And YOU'RE a particularly hot property at the moment, Liam. There's been a lot of things going on and there will be again. We want you back when the time's right. In the meantime it's play it safe. Alright?

LIAM: Orders is orders. For how long will it be?

FRANKIE: Now you know better than to ask that. But we'll be in touch. Shouldn't be too long.

JOE: When are we to leave?

FRANKIE: The night.

JOE: The night?

FRANKIE: That's what I said. It's all organized. Everybody knows what's what. So there's nothing to worry about. Just keep your wits about you until you're across the border. And after!

JOE: I haven't been in Dublin since just after the troubles started. Remember that time, Liam, we went down for that demo about housing.

LIAM: Aye. Preserve the front facades of Dublin's Georgian houses. Jesus, those were the days!

FRANKIE: Aye, well you both had other things to occupy you since, aside from architecture.

LIAM: Christ! When you think about it. It's fuckin' amazing. And it doesn't seem all that long ago.

JOE: Fourteen years, Liam. That's all!

FRANKIE: O.K., lads. Yiz know the score. All the best. And good luck!

JOE: Right, Frankie. All the best.

LIAM: Don't forget about us now, Frankie. Remember where we are, won't you?

FRANKIE: Away on with the both of ye!

Exit Frankie.
Cross-fade to Liam and Joe. As if travelling in car.
Pause.

JOE: Were you ever in Dublin when you were a kid, Liam?

LIAM: Aye. A few times.

JOE: Did yiz go on the train?

LIAM: Catholic building trade workers didn't have cars. Aye. We went on the special excursion.

JOE: And do you remember anything special about the train stopping at Drogheda?

LIAM: Aye. My mother used to tell us to say a prayer for the canonization of Blessed Oliver Plunkett.

JOE: My mother used to say the same.

LIAM: We must have been quare pray-ers in those days, Joe. For it worked. Isn't he a saint now?

JOE: Yeh. I think he was elevated to sainthood there by our Polish comrade.

LIAM: I'm surprised he didn't canonize Oliver Cromwell instead. But here, do you remember throwing pennies out of the train —

JOE: — when it was going over the Drogheda bridge.

LIAM: And you had to make three wishes.

JOE: I wonder what the fuck all that was about?

LIAM: We both must've had mothers who were inclined towards Paganism!

JOE: Have you ever known an Irish mother who wasn't?

LIAM: You know, Joe, you might have something there. For I remember my mother always talking about holy wells and ancient Mass stones that had once been the graves of Celtic goddesses and visiting cairns in Sligo.

JOE: And fairy forts and magic circles and hiding behind the couch and being doused in Lourdes water whenever there was thunder and lightning. Oh, it could never be a 'simple' faith they had!

LIAM: Aye. But I'll tell you one thing, Joe. I bet you it never crossed their minds that twenty odd years later their two sons would be driving in the direction of Dublin's fair city — ON THE RUN!

Blackout/music.

SCENE 4

Lights up slowly.
Dublin. A 'safe' house.
We see Liam and Joe. Both lying on single beds. Silence.
Liam jumps up and lights cigarette, agitated.

LIAM: Is it a week now, Joe?

JOE: A week the morrow.

LIAM: Christ, is that all? Seems like a fuckin' eternity.

JOE: Take it easy, will ye, Liam.

LIAM: Take it easy? What do you think I've been doing? Holed up here in this fuckin' 'safe' house in the arse end of Dublin. We haven't been doing much else now, have we?

JOE: That's the orders, Liam.

LIAM: Yes. I know, Joe. That's the orders. But it doesn't stop me feeling pissed off. Doing nothing. Hanging about. Passing the fuckin' time. Playing cards.

JOE: Do you fancy a game?

LIAM: No! I fuckin' do not. And if you bring them out again I'll ram them down your bloody throat.

JOE: I like cards myself.

LIAM: Joe!

Pause.

JOE: What's the problem, Liam? I've never seen you get rattled like this before and we've been through a brave bit.

LIAM: Ah nothing, Joe. I just hate this inactivity.

JOE: Well, you've had plenty of action recently. And no doubt you'll have a lot more, going on what Frankie was saying.

LIAM: I know. No doubt. But it's not just that.

JOE: What then? The woman?

LIAM: Neh. Sure I hardly ever saw her when I was in Belfast. An hour here and an hour there.

JOE: Romantic that.

LIAM: Aye. Very. You can explain that to her when you next see her.

JOE: Well, if it's not the woman?

LIAM: You're going to kill yourself at this!

JOE: I'm waiting.

LIAM: It's — Belfast. I miss Belfast.

JOE: God, I thought you were going to tell me something there. So what's surprising about that? You think I don't.

LIAM: Do you, Joe?

JOE: Of course I fuckin' do. It's never out of my mind. I dream about it. And when I'm awake, different places — parts of it keep popping up. It's always there in front of me. I even get pleasure from picturing the streets at this time of the night . . . even with the Brit patrols knocking about. It's like they're a part of it all, part of Belfast . . . and I want to keep the scene, the picture, in my head.

LIAM: And it's not just the Brits. For I keep thinking of the Loyalists as well. I nearly get a warm glow thinking of Orange processions. And the Shankill Road keeps appearing to me. I can see Peter's Hill and the Protestant flats. And all those wee Protestant men and women and their children — all in their homes — having their tea, watching the news and F-ing and blinding about us Fenians and especially cursing people the likes of us and you know, Joe . . . I . . . I . . .

JOE: LOVE it?

LIAM: Aye. That's what it is. Love. I fuckin' love all of it . . . the whole fuckin' messed up shit heap that other people see it as.

JOE: Who? The Brits, Liam?

LIAM: The Brits for one. AND the Free Staters down here for another. But it's Belfast: that's what Belfast is. That's what makes it. It's what makes us, Joe.

JOE: And yet you and I are fighting to change it, Liam?

LIAM: Aye. I know. And look at us! Fighting to change it means we end up here in Dublin and hating the fact that we're here.

JOE: And yet this is the place we're fighting to join up with, Liam.

LIAM: Oh fuck, Joe, I know. And sometimes I wonder why? For everything I hear and see tells me we're a very different people. And the fact that Fenians like you and I are having 'visions' of the Shankill Road and NOT Dublin's O'Connell Street is saying something. But it doesn't mean I'm not for blowing the Brits across the water — I am — but I just wish to God that more of those wee Protestant men and women would start seeing the Falls, start seeing us in a very different light. We're all from the North!

Enter the Gardai . . . Irish Special Branch Police.

OFFICER: Alright lads. HOLD IT!

Special Branch Officers have guns trained on Liam and Joe.
Hold.
Blackout.

5   SCENE

The London flat of Elizabeth and Roy. Elizabeth is a writer and historian and Roy is a Left Wing Member of the Labour Party. Steven, Roy's friend and also a Labour M.P., has been invited to Dinner.

Lights up.
All three have a drink in hand.

ROY: Well, cheers everybody!

STEVEN: Cheers!

Elizabeth just raises her glass nonchantly as they toast each other.
Pause.

ELIZABETH: Roy tells me you've been on a Party fact-finding mission in Belfast, Steven?

STEVEN: Yes. I've just got back. Well, it's nearly a week but I feel as if I'm still recovering from it.

ELIZABETH: Recovering? Was it that debilitating?

ROY: Yes. How was it, Steven? I haven't had a chance to talk to you about it. Saw you in the corridor whatever day it was but had no time to stop. Select Committee meeting I think it was.

ELIZABETH: You were about to answer my question, Steven.

STEVEN: Yes. Well. It wasn't exactly debilitating, Elizabeth, but it was illuminating. Very illuminating!

ELIZABETH: Really, in what way?

ROY: Your first visit was it, Steven?

STEVEN: Yes. As a matter of fact it was. I'd always meant to go before but somehow it had just never happened. I wish I had now. Of course you have been on a number of occasions, Roy, haven't you?

ROY: No. Never. Never set foot in Ireland — let alone Belfast. Nearly went on holiday to Kerry once — supposed to be quite beautiful you know — but I never quite made it.

STEVEN: Really? Why did I think you'd been then? Perhaps I'd assumed it, given our many conversations on the North.

ELIZABETH: ILLUMINATING!

ROY: What's that Elizabeth?

ELIZABETH: Steven was saying how 'illuminating' his fact-finding trip to Belfast was.

ROY: Oh, I'm sorry, Steve. Interrupting your flow. Refills, everybody?

Drinks business.

ELIZABETH: So, in what way was it illuminating, Steve?

STEVEN: Have you ever been, Elizabeth?

ELIZABETH: No. Which is why I'm keen to hear how you found it.

STEVEN: Grim. Very grim indeed.

ROY: It's as bad as they say then, Steven?

STEVEN: I'm not sure what THEY say but it is pretty bloody awful. And I'm ashamed to think how we could've let it go on for so long. I mean, how people have put up with it for fifteen years defeats me. As I say, it was not only illuminating . . . it shook me somewhat. The city of Belfast itself has the feel of one huge Maze Prison . . . doesn't matter whether it's a Protestant or Catholic area you're in. The ghettoes are like compounds and the city centre riddled with Security Gates. Checkpoints. Soldiers. If that's not a war landscape then I don't know what is. The word 'troubles' seems a little less than apt to describe that situation.

ELIZABETH: It was 'depressingly' illuminating then, Steven?

STEVEN: It certainly depressed me to think that we on the Left in Britain have allowed it to continue, indeed perpetuated the repression. For that's what it is — REPRESSION.

ROY: Our record certainly hasn't been too admirable in Ireland that's for sure, Steven. But things are changing, are they not? I mean we are beginning to realize that we haven't been doing right.

STEVEN: Christ. I hope so, Roy. And not before time if you ask me. I mean, how could we have called ourselves socialists all these years and allowed that bloody dire situation to continue is almost beyond me. It IS beyond me. Yes, we can say we put forward motions at Conference. That we tried. And when we did try we had mud thrown at us from the Press, the Tories, from our own Right Wing and centre. But we are supposed to be the Left, Roy. We are supposed to be anti-imperialist.

ROY: We are, Steven.

STEVEN: Anti-colonialist . . .

ROY: We are.

STEVEN: Anti-racist . . .

ROY: We are.

STEVEN: Supporters of Irish national freedom?

ROY: For all our faults and limitations, we are, Steven.

STEVEN: Well, why the hell, then, haven't we acted upon it before now? Why have we been content to sit back and hope it would just go away . . . ? Disappear . . . ? This complication to our parliamentary lives that we really didn't want to have to bother about. It's a crying bloody shame, Roy. And we should hang our heads at the very thought of it.

ROY: I'm not proud of our treatment of Ireland, Steven. And I think we have a lot to answer for . . .

STEVEN: I'm sorry, Roy, I wasn't meaning to get at you. Like I said, the Belfast trip was something of an eye-opener for me. Maybe Elizabeth's right. I am debilitated by it.

ROY: You certainly seem to have been moved by it, Steve. But, I repeat, I'm not proud of our Northern Ireland record and I agree with everything you've said. It's not that we shouldn't take action — do something — I agree we should but it's the nature of that action that troubles me. What kind of action should we take? What can we do? What is it that will positively improve the lot of the people in Northern Ireland? Action. Yes. But it must be action that moves things forward; benefits the working-class of both communities; helps them identify with the class interests of each other. And the way to do that is not always as clear as we would like it to be, Steve.

STEVEN: Isn't it?

ROY: I don't think it is.

STEVEN: Well, I do, Roy. For I believe there is no other answer to the problem than a clear commitment from us. A policy statement to the effect that Ireland will be united within a certain set time. Troops out, and structures formed to facilitate that action within the set period and a handing over of the North to the Government of the day in Dublin. We were wrong, Roy, wrong to partition the country. We then allowed a neo-fascist Unionist Party to misrule for over fifty years and for the last ten years of Direct Rule we have systematically impeded the struggle of a people for national freedom. Troops out, it must be, if we are to continue to call ourselves socialists!

ELIZABETH: Anyone for dinner?

Hold/blackout.

SCENE   6

Belfast. The home of a working class Protestant/Loyalist family.

We see Derek and his mother, Mrs. Smith. Derek is packing a suitcase.

MOTHER: God, Derek, son, I never thought I'd see the day you HAD to leave Belfast to find work in England.

DEREK: Aye, Ma. Well there it is. I do. It's 1984 and even we Ulster Loyalists have to take the Liverpool boat.

MOTHER: I mean, your father HAD to in the thirties but I never thought you would have to as well. I could see you going for the break or if you wanted to get away from this place for a while but out of your own choice. NOT HAVING TO!

DEREK: Oh, I know Ma. But the building game in Northern Ireland is not what it was. People like me are getting paid off every Friday now. It's Taigs and Prods are getting their cards these days.

MOTHER: Is there nothing doing, son? Are you sure you couldn't get fixed up somewhere?

DEREK: Oh, no doubt, Ma, eventually I could. If I decided to play ball with those building sites that still have work. But no way am I handing over a percentage of what I've sweated for to you know who! I'll do many's the thing for them but I'm not paying to be allowed to work. My Da never did and I think that's a family tradition worth keeping.

MOTHER: Is Sam going with you?

DEREK: He is.

MOTHER: Well, at least you'll have company. I'd hate to think of you going over to London on your own. People say it's an awful lonely, unfriendly place, you know. Will yiz get digs or what?

DEREK: Ma, don't you be worrying your head about us. We'll get fixed up alright. Sam's been over before and knows the score. He has a few contacts and we're going to check out the landlady he stayed with. He said it was great. She even used to bake soda bread and everything. It wasn't like ours but it wasn't a bad substitute.

MOTHER: Aye. Well you make sure you get your grub alright. Good grub and enough of it, for you can't go building brick with nothing in your stomach of a morning.

DEREK: Ma, will you stop worrying. Have you ever known me to go hungry?

MOTHER: No. But you've always had your Ma to make sure you didn't. It mightn't have been steak every night but your father and you always had a good feed morning and night and a sandwich lunch in your pocket that would have fed many's a regiment on the march.

DEREK: Oh, I know, Ma. But I'll not starve. Don't you worry. What's the right time?

MOTHER: It's after seven, Derek. Have you got your tools and all with you?

DEREK: I have.

MOTHER: And are you sure you have enough money?

DEREK: Yes, Ma. More than enough. Listen, I'll ring the morrow as soon as we've arrived and got sorted out with the accommodation.

MOTHER: Make sure you do now, Derek. For I'll be worried sick until I hear from you. And promise me, son, you'll watch your step, won't you? And if Sam gets out of line, don't you put your hand in the fire as well. Just take the first boat and come home. You'd maybe get something here. Ye never know!

DEREK: Ma, it's England I'm going to not the Siberian salt mines. I'm a tradesman prepared to work. I'm a Protestant. I have me British passport and things are going to be alright. Now, will you for God's sake quit going on.

MOTHER: But, Derek . . .

DEREK: That'll be Sam. Right Ma, all the best. You take care and look after yourself and, as I say, I'll ring you immediately I arrive.

MOTHER: How are yiz getting down to the boat?

DEREK: Oh, Sam's brother is running us down in the motor. Right then, I'm away. Take care now. You hear, Ma.

Exit Derek.

MOTHER: And you, take care, son.

Hold/blackout.

7 SCENE

Slow cross-fade to Derek and Sam on deck of Liverpool boat. We hear ship's horn. Boat is pulling away from harbour. They are looking back at city of Belfast.

SAM: Well, there she goes, Derek. We're off. Au revoir, Belfast! All the best!

DEREK: Aye. We're off.

SAM: Do you see the Albert clock still? Thonder on the left.

DEREK: Aye. And the rain pissing down on Great George's Street and York Street.

SAM: And the top of Gallagher's tobacco factory. Can you see it?

DEREK: Oh, for a dreg of a Gallagher's green or blue.

SAM: And look, Derek, do you see the lights of the houses on the Shore road?

DEREK: My sister and I used to walk along the Shore road counting the Christmas trees in the windows when we were kids.

SAM: There's people in those wee houses with the lights on.

DEREK: All having their dinner and watching the news. And . . . Come on, you can buy me that pint you were talking about!

Blackout. Music. Sound.

London. A grotty bedsit in Paddington. Enter Derek and Sam. They have just returned from work on building site.

DEREK: How long have we been here now, Sam? In the Big Smoke?

SAM: Almost three months, Derek. Why?

DEREK: Ah nothing. It just feels sometimes like it's been three years.

SAM: What's wrong with you? Are you missing your Ma? Or has a great passion come over you for potato bread and a big Ulster fry?

DEREK: Oh, fuck off, you.

SAM: It wasn't my fault that the landlady I had the first time committed suicide!

DEREK: I wonder how long it was after you'd left that she did it? (*Pause*) No. No jesting, Sam. I mean, I've witnessed the effect you can have on women. I mean, I know you can't help it. But it's — cruel — I mean, just to withdraw like that, and remove that smile from their world.

SAM: There's somebody in here looking for a kick in the kitter if they're not careful.

DEREK: Aye. You see. And then threatening violence at the mention of the truth.

SAM: There could've been blood spilt all over the 'thick pile' carpet of this luxurious box we pay fifty quid a week for.

DEREK: You know, that fuckin' landlord must make a thousand a week out of this house alone with the rents he's charging.

And I'm sure it's not the only property he owns. It's quare money for doing nothing. And I think of what we get with overtime and bonuses for building the bloody houses. There's something wrong with that equation, you know, Sam.

SAM: I suppose you'll be going home to join forces with Bernadette Devlin soon the way you're talking.

DEREK: Aye. Maybe I will.

SAM: And am I to expect you to get up on Sunday morning to go to Mass with the Dublin and Cork navvies as well?

DEREK: You'd have problems there, Sam. For I don't think there's too many of them tread that path themselves.

SAM: Well, you could set the example, Derek!

DEREK: No, but Sam, don't you think it's a fuckin' odd do that here we are: Prods from Belfast working away with Taigs from the North and the South of Ireland in London, England! All of us living in digs or rooms like this that we're paying through the nose for?

SAM: We've worked with Taigs at home, Derek. You and I haven't been on a site these past five years that didn't have a mixed work force.

DEREK: Aye. Mixed. But with us in a solid majority. And both lots heading for their respective ghettoes come knocking off time.

SAM: Well, how could it be any different, Derek, given the way things are at home.

DEREK: I don't know, Sam. But it's fuckin' different here. We're in a minority! And we're all living in the same appalling fuckin' conditions — Taigs and Prods! We eat in the same cafés. We drink in the same pubs. And we both have to walk through the same shit on the site!

SAM: Oh, the shit on building sites, Derek, isn't any different no matter what side of the water you're on.

DEREK: But Sam, the point is, why are we all here in the first place? Why are the Kerry men here? Why are the Cork men here? The Dublin men? The Falls road men? And us, from the Shankill? And why, on a site where the majority of men working — tradesmen and labourers, all of them from some or other part of Ireland — why is it that the fuckin' foreman is an Englishman?

SAM: Derek, you're beginning to talk like a Fenian!

DEREK: Ah Sam, you can geag about it, but one thing is becoming very clear to me. You might be British or a Loyalist when you're in the six counties but once you get off that Liverpool boat or emerge from Euston station, to the Englishman . . . WE'RE ALL PADDIES! And he doesn't distinguish between the Taig or Prod sort. In fact, if anything, he seems to get on better with the Kerry or Cork man than he does with us who are British from the North.

SAM: Maybe he knows them better since they've been coming over for longer.

DEREK: Aye. And maybe he doesn't want to know us at all!

Pause.
Exchange looks.
Blackout.

SCENE 9

Lights up.
Scene as at end of previous scene at Bishop's Palace. We see the Bishop, Father Crilly, and Father Quinn.

BISHOP: Good morning, Father Quinn. Nice to see you again.

FATHER QUINN: Good morning, Your Eminence. (*Kisses ring of Bishop*) Father Crilly.

FATHER CRILLY: Father Quinn.

BISHOP: Well, take a seat. Make yourself comfortable. Perhaps you'd like a cup of tea? Or coffee? I'm sorry, Father Crilly, I didn't offer you anything when you arrived.

FATHER CRILLY: No. Your Eminence. I'm fine. I drink too much tea as it is.

FATHER QUINN: Not for me either, Your Eminence, thank you.

BISHOP: And it's a little early for sherry, gentlemen. Don't you think?

FATHER CRILLY: Quite. Your Eminence.

BISHOP: We'd have my housekeeper 'wondering' if she came in to find the three of us sitting at ten o'clock in the morning with glasses in our hands.

FATHER CRILLY: We would, Your Eminence (*chuckles*).

Father Quinn smiles.

BISHOP: Well, Father Quinn, how are things? Father Crilly was telling me that building on the new school is progressing at a great rate altogether.

FATHER QUINN: Yes, Your Eminence. It certainly seems to be going ahead remarkably smoothly.

FATHER CRILLY: Oh, I think it'll be ready in time for opening in September as planned, Your Eminence.

BISHOP: That's grand. All we have to do now is find the money to pay for it.

FATHER CRILLY: The debt is slowly diminishing, Your Eminence. The people of the parish have been very generous in their offerings.

BISHOP: Well, they know it's themselves it'll benefit . . . or at least their children. For God knows, in these times, a good Catholic education is certainly needed. Wouldn't you agree, Father Quinn?

FATHER QUINN: I would certainly agree with that, Your Eminence. Education is very much what our people need on a whole range of subjects especially in these times, as you say.

BISHOP: Yes (*glances at Father Crilly*). Quite. Well, Father Crilly, I think we should get down to the business in hand without further delay. Don't you?

FATHER CRILLY: Yes. Your Eminence, I think we should.

BISHOP: Father Quinn, I expect you have an inkling of an idea as to why this meeting is taking place this morning?

FATHER QUINN: More than an inkling perhaps, Your Eminence.

BISHOP: Yes, Father Quinn. It is a kind of further chapter to the previous discussions we have had on this same subject.

FATHER QUINN: About the newspaper column, Your Eminence.

BISHOP: That is the very subject, Father Quinn, to which I am referring (*indicates paper*). Now, this latest piece has given cause for Father Crilly and me to feel a certain disquiet over the matter. And, we were wondering what you felt or thought about the situation yourself?

FATHER QUINN: With respect, Your Eminence, I'm a little surprised that you or Father Crilly should feel such disquiet.

BISHOP: Are you now, Father Quinn?

FATHER QUINN: Well, with respect, Your Eminence, I don't think the newspaper article should be a cause for disquiet. Discussion, yes, but not disquiet or worry.

BISHOP: Well, I should tell you then, Father Quinn, that I am worried, as I think Father Crilly is.

FATHER CRILLY: Father Quinn, I think it is a matter for serious concern.

FATHER QUINN: And I would agree Father Crilly, the whole subject and the issues I have raised in that article are very much a matter for serious concern; which is why I wrote the piece in the first place.

BISHOP: Let me ask you, Father Quinn, what was your purpose in writing the piece? What do you hope to achieve by this?

FATHER QUINN: Stimulation of thought. Open discussion. An exchange, perhaps, in the letters column of the paper, with people in the area, in the parish, writing and thinking about it.

FATHER CRILLY: (*Angry*) Encourage people to attack the Church, you mean, Father Quinn.

FATHER QUINN: I don't see that prompting discussion is necessarily attacking, Father Crilly.

FATHER CRILLY: Don't you?

BISHOP: But isn't that what you yourself have done, Father Quinn? Attack!

FATHER QUINN: I don't agree, Your Eminence.

BISHOP: (*Quoting paper*) 'Is the Church or some of its ministers out of step if not out of sympathy with its flock on the realities of Northern Ireland politics?' I don't know about Father Crilly, but that to me reads like an attack and a fairly full-blooded one at that.

FATHER CRILLY: I would agree entirely, Your Eminence.

FATHER QUINN: And I would say, Father Crilly, Your Eminence, that it is as you read it. Is the Church out of step? I ask the question. I don't make a statement.

BISHOP: Oh damn it, man, don't play semantics. You may phrase it so but you know damn rightly, as we do, how people will read it — how the Government will read it!

FATHER CRILLY: As a minister of the Church — a priest — attacking the Church, that's how they'll read it. You wouldn't do this, Father Quinn, only you know there are some among the community who agree with those sentiments. And here they are. Now they have a Catholic priest leading the onslaught.

FATHER QUINN: Oh, come now, Father Crilly. Don't you think that's a slight exaggeration — 'Onslaught'?

BISHOP: No. Father Quinn. I don't think it is.

FATHER QUINN: But, Your Eminence. If such a thing can be described as an onslaught — when what we're talking about is raising a question for discussion — does that not prove my point, that such issues as I do raise are crying out for debate and argument? Is it not better that we air them rather than try to shield ourselves behind vindictive authority? I'm not referring to you, Your Eminence, or Father Crilly in that.

BISHOP: I'm grateful for that, Father Quinn. As I'm sure Father Crilly is. Perhaps, then, it is time that we, or rather you, 'aired' these issues more fully now. Perhaps we should hear your answer, Father Quinn, to the question you've raised.

Pause.

FATHER CRILLY: We're waiting, Father Quinn.

Hold. Blackout.

Lights up.
Dublin. A police interview room.
We see Liam and an officer of the Dublin Special Branch. S.B. man
is in fifties.

Pause.

OFFICER: You're an idealist, Liam. I can see that. And sure so was
my own father. He was an idealist too. And wasn't he shot
through the head for his trouble by his fellow countrymen
during the Civil War? That's what idealism got him, Liam.
Oh, and he was on the right side as you would see it — he
was anti-treaty. But, as I see it, Liam, the only right side to
be on is the side that wins. And you, Liam, have the look of
a loser and so do those like you. You're all born losers! You
see, Liam, we've had our War of Independence and we've
had our Civil War too. And you see, Liam, we're going to
make damn sure we don't have any more. We HAVE a
Republic of Ireland. And we don't like its peace and quiet
being disturbed by the likes of you, or by Loyalist bombs
because your Protestant friends in the North get upset by
the antics that you and your comrades indulge in. You
could say, Liam, to be perfectly frank about it, we know
what side our bread's buttered on, now that we have the
bread. And you are being very foolish in your idealism if
you think that 'our' Republic of Ireland is going to join
forces with the likes of you. In fact, Liam, you're pissing in
the wind, if you think for one second that we here in the
South are interested in you at all, let alone wanting you to
join us OR take over in the formation of a 32 County

Socialist Republic. The country of Ireland will be united in time, but it hasn't got any time or space for you or what you want. And as it happened to idealists in the past we will, in true De Valera fashion, put you and your kind up against the wall and make collanders of you! Do you get my meaning, Liam?

LIAM: Oh, I get the message alright. You gombeen bastard!

Officer goes to hit Liam. Blackout.

11 SCENE

London. A building site. We see Derek reading a newspaper. Enter Ron, the Cockney foreman.

RON: Slacking are we, Paddy?

DEREK: Yeh. Coming now, Sam.

RON: Well, you better fuckin' hurry up.

Ron snatches paper from Derek who turns to see it is Ron, the foreman.

DEREK: Oh, it's you, Ron. I thought it was my mate, Sam, geaging about.

Derek puts out hand for paper.

RON: No. It's not Sam geaging about. Sam's over where you should be.

DEREK: Eh?

RON: On the scaffold, mate. Building brick. Working!

DEREK: Can I have my paper back please, Ron?

RON: I thought I'd warned you before about time-keeping. This isn't the first time, mate.

DEREK: What are you going on about? There's five minutes yet to starting time. Now can I have that paper?

RON: My watch says it's five minutes after starting time. And you can have your paper AFTER knocking off time. Maybe. In the meantime, I want you over on that scaffold. Working. There's no slacking on this job, you know. You're not at home in the bogs now.

DEREK: Are you serious, Ron?

RON: Never more serious in my life. Now get a fuckin' move on will you, Paddy.

DEREK: Well, you know what you can do, don't you, MATE? Now, give me that fuckin' paper before . . .

RON: Before what, Paddy? I'm the foreman around here and I give the orders.

DEREK: The name's Derek as a matter of fact.

RON: Oh, Derek is it? You think you're different do you? Well, I say it's Paddy and. . .

DEREK: Listen, why don't you just go and fuck yourself, Mr. English foreman?

RON: You fuckin' Irish bastard!

Ron lunges at Derek who sidesteps and trips him. Ron falls. He hits his head on iron girder. He doesn't move. Derek goes to him. Shakes him.

DEREK: Hey, pal. Come on. Quit coding.

Derek rolls him over.

DEREK: OH FUCK!!

Blackout. Music.

Interval.

Lights up.
Scene as in scene 2. The Bishop's residence. We see Bishop, Father Crilly and Father Quinn.

BISHOP: Well now, Father Quinn. The floor is yours. And Father Crilly and myself are waiting and listening.

FATHER QUINN: Your Eminence. Father Crilly. There is, I feel, one issue above all others which we as ministers of the Church need to address ourselves to . . . that is not to say that we haven't in the past, for we have — consistently. Public statements have been made, sermons have been preached and more. Personal communications in the confessional, in the homes of parishioners, wherever, all this has been done. But the manner and form of these pronouncements I would suggest needs revising.

BISHOP: And, before Father Crilly and I explode with the suspense of it all, what IS this issue, Father Quinn?

FATHER QUINN: It's the subject of violence.

FATHER CRILLY: I thought so.

BISHOP: Let's hear what he has to say, Father Crilly.

FATHER QUINN: Well, Your Eminence, I feel, and I've given the matter some considerable thought, that it is not enough for us — priests — just to go on condemning the violence of the people.

FATHER CRILLY: Not all our people subscribe to violence, Father Quinn.

FATHER QUINN: No. Father Crilly. And I wasn't for a second

suggesting that they do. But there are those, and in our parish, Father Crilly, who, if they don't actually carry out acts of violence themselves, do support and sympathize, albeit in a passive way, with those that do.

BISHOP: Yes, Father Quinn. And recent events would seem to confirm that assertion, I'm sorry to say.

FATHER QUINN: Yes, Your Eminence, they would. Now, I'm not saying that violence should not be condemned. It must be. Murder is murder! It is a mortal sin against God whatever the motivation or provocation. But what I am saying is that murder is murder and must be condemned, no matter who commits it. Violence or killing by the authorities — the army, the loyalist paramilitaries — IS also violence, also MURDER!

FATHER CRILLY: There's no one would deny that, Father Quinn. And we have condemned it. Condemned it out of hand.

BISHOP: And been criticized for so doing, Father Quinn. The number of phone calls I've had from the Northern Ireland office on this very matter and from the press and television! The whole thing is an issue that requires incredibly delicate handling, Father Quinn.

FATHER QUINN: I appreciate that, Your Eminence.

BISHOP: Do you, Father Quinn?

FATHER QUINN: Yes, I do. But what I'm concerned about is that our people do not always see, rightly or wrongly, that our stand on what I will call violence from the establishment is as strong or un-equivocal as that when we condemn violence against the establishment.

FATHER CRILLY: And those that believe that, Father Quinn, will be the very ones that are perpetuating the violence — the I.R.A.!

FATHER QUINN: But are they not also our people, our parishioners, Father Crilly?

FATHER CRILLY: Yes, of course they are, but that is exactly why we must condemn 'their' violence.

FATHER QUINN: Father Crilly, it is a fact that throughout Irish history, the Church, nine times out of ten, has sided with the establishment. With the English Government!

FATHER CRILLY: And there have been times in Irish history, Father Quinn, when Catholic priests themselves have been 'on the run' from the English authorities. For saying the Mass!

FATHER QUINN: I do not deny that, Father Crilly. But the people also know that the Church's record in taking a stand against English oppression is not a good one and we, the priests today, by not speaking out against the authorities, are not changing that old record.

BISHOP: But Father Quinn, we have spoken out. Your premise has no foundation.

FATHER QUINN: But, Your Eminence, not strongly enough. And as I've said, rightly or wrongly, there is a climate of opinion among our people that we display a reticence in the face of violence from the authorities. And I fear that if we do not remedy that situation the people will increasingly turn away from us. They will leave the Church. Stop practising. There is, as it stands, a duality amongst them — a split worship — the Catholic church versus Cathleen Ni Houlihan.

BISHOP: The Pagan Goddess!

FATHER QUINN: Precisely, Your Eminence. And let us not forget that the Irish people are perhaps more pagan than we sometimes care to think.

BISHOP: The old mythologies are still alive, you mean, Father Quinn?

FATHER QUINN: And our Catholic Ireland is but a thin gloss on a Pagan underworld.

FATHER CRILLY: Oh, come on! Begging your pardon, Your Eminence, but Ireland has been a Christian country since 426 A.D. and today is one of the countries of the world where Roman Catholicism is most strong. It's renowned for it. Go abroad and mention Ireland and people will see it as almost synonymous with Catholicism — apart from a small section of the Protestant population here in the North.

FATHER QUINN: Is it so strong, Father Crilly? And if it is, why then do 'our Catholic population' behave as they do in spite of, and in direct contradiction to, our teachings? We condemn their acts of violence but it doesn't stop them from carrying out these acts in the name of what His Eminence so rightly calls 'the Pagan Goddess'!

FATHER CRILLY: But this is ridiculous. I've never heard so much nonsense.

BISHOP: No. Father Crilly. I don't think it is.

FATHER CRILLY: Your Eminence. . .

BISHOP: I think our Father Quinn here has a very good point. The behaviour of our people does display a dual allegiance, a kind of schizophrenia. Christian v. Pagan. Mind you, I think it applies only to this part of Ireland. If you'll forgive me, gentlemen, for saying it, this province of Ulster has always been troublesomely askew, to put it mildly. And it has nothing to do with the Protestants. They're just another complication in what has always been 'a world apart'. Is it any wonder there's trouble when we have a wild Ulster paganism with a layer of Catholicism on top of it and another layer of free-wheeling Paisleyite Presbyterianism on top of that again? Sure it's a recipe for chaos and madness.

FATHER QUINN: And if you'll forgive me, Your Eminence, it's because of all this that I feel it is in our interests, or rather in the interests of the Catholic Church, to ensure that we do not alienate, more than they already are, our people! We must be extremely careful in our handling of them. For at the end of the day, and it does not matter which day, we can be fairly certain that the English presence in Ireland will finally come to an end . . . and our job is surely to ensure that when that happens (*Pause*) our Roman Catholic churches are still full. And it is the Pagan Goddess who is feebly searching for worshippers.

Pause.

BISHOP: Father Quinn. There's obviously more to you than meets the eye.

Bishop and Father Quinn smile knowingly.
Father Crilly looks perplexed.
Slow fade. Music.

13 | SCENE

London. The interview room of a police station.
We see Derek.
Pause.
Enter plain-clothes detective (S.B.).

DEREK: Any news from the hospital, Detective?

DETECTIVE: Nothing new, Mr. Smith. No change. He's still on the danger list, I'm afraid.

Derek sinks into chair.

Pause.

DEREK: Jesus!

DETECTIVE: O.K. Mr. Smith. Let's go through it once more.

DEREK: But Detective, we've been through it . . . over and over again. We've been through it a hundred bloody times.

DETECTIVE: And we may have to go through it another hundred, Mr. Smith.

DEREK: But it doesn't change. It's just the same. It's exactly as I've told it to you. He took a swing at me. I sidestepped, tripped him and he fell. And he hit his head on the . . .

DETECTIVE: On the what, Mr Smith?

DEREK: On this bloody oul rusty iron girder that was lying sticking out. It wasn't my fault. It was an accident. Could've happened to anybody! It could've happened to you, Detective.

DETECTIVE: But it didn't, Mr. Smith. It happened to you.

DEREK: Aye. I know. It happened to me alright. Look, Detective, what's my situation here? I mean, I can't be charged with anything if it was an accident, if it was self defence, now can I?

DETECTIVE: IF it was accident. IF it was self defence, Mr. Smith.

DEREK: But it was. I've told you it was. What do you mean 'IF'?

DETECTIVE: Mr. Smith, there were no witnesses to this event. Your friend, Sam Wilson, arrived after the 'action'.

DEREK: Yes, I know, but . . .

DETECTIVE   But nothing! The situation is this: a man is in hospital, he is on the danger list and he is there as a result of an incident involving you.

DEREK: Yes. But . . .

DETECTIVE: How long have you been in England, Mr. Smith?

DEREK: Just over three months.

DETECTIVE: And why did you come over?

DEREK: For work. Things are bad at home. I was paid off the job I was on.

DETECTIVE: Why?

DEREK: What do you mean 'why'?

DETECTIVE: I mean why were you asked to leave your last job in Belfast?

DEREK: I wasn't asked to leave, Detective. I was paid off. There was no more work. The job we were on was finished.

DETECTIVE: I see. And so you decided to come to England to seek work?

DEREK: Yes. That's what I just said. Detective, what has all this got to do with . . .

DETECTIVE: Mr. Smith, are you a member of any political organization?

DEREK: WHAT?

DETECTIVE: In Northern Ireland?

DEREK: No.

DETECTIVE: Am I right in thinking, Mr. Smith, that you are a Protestant from Belfast?

DEREK: Yes.

DETECTIVE: Are you what some might call a LOYALIST, Mr. Smith?

DEREK: Eh? What is this? What's that got to do with anything?

DETECTIVE: It may have a lot to do with some things, Mr. Smith. Now, answer my question. Are you a LOYALIST?

DEREK: I'm British, if that's what you mean, Detective.

DETECTIVE: But that's not what I mean, Mr. Smith, for the two are not necessarily the same.

DEREK: Well, I'm sorry, Detective but they are to me. I'm British and I'm loyal to the Crown. So that makes a LOYALIST. LOYALIST. BRITISH. But what has any of this to do with what happened on the job the day?

DETECTIVE: That's what I'd like to find out. (*Pause*) Don't go away, Mr. Smith.

> *Detective exits.*
> *Hold on Derek. Blackout.*
> *Music.*

14 SCENE

The London Flat.
We see Elizabeth, Roy and Steven. Dinner is over and they are having coffee.

ELIZABETH: More coffee, comrades?

STEVEN: No thanks, Elizabeth. And thank you for such a splendid meal.

ROY: But Steven, I don't think there are many British people in the country who would disagree with you, albeit for different reasons. I think if you asked every member of the

Party, even those on the far Right, whether Ireland should, in theory, be united, they would undoubtedly say yes. But, at the end of the day, Steven, it still comes back to the old thorny question: What about the Protestants? The Unionists? The Loyalists? Call them what the hell you like — the fact remains, they will say 'NO' to a United Ireland. They have historically and consistently said 'NO'. They have taken up arms to show that they mean 'NO' when they say it and it will take a better man than me to say that they will not do so again. If we withdraw troops, hint that we may consider doing so, what happens? The spectre of bloody civil war stares us in the face. We do have a responsibility, Steve.

STEVEN: Yes, Roy. We have a responsibility. A responsibility to get out. To get out of a country we should never have been in — and once in, stayed in for far far too long. It's the last colony, Roy. And only 200 miles away! We have given up many others much further away; ask the good Lord Carrington.

ROY: Yes, Steven. Yes. I know. And I agree. And every time we said we never would we always did. But you haven't answered my question. The imminent Civil War, the blood bath, Steven, what of our responsibility regarding that?

STEVEN: It's a myth, Roy. An English myth. And even if it's not — so what? What's the difference between that and what we've got now? Over two thousand civilian Irish people have died since 1968. Nearly 800 members of the security forces. 24,000 human beings have been injured or maimed — and still the slow tortuous saga continues.

ROY: But won't it even be worse if we pull out, Steven? How many more thousands will die in the hand-to-hand, street-to-street fighting of the bloodiest of civil wars?

STEVEN: And how many more thousands, Roy, will continue to die under the Direct Rule of the British Government of whatever bloody party? We're not solving anything by the easy option of an 'acceptable level of violence'. How cynical is that phrase? 'Acceptable violence'. It doesn't matter if you die Sean O'Brien or Corporal Smith; for if you didn't even more would! I think Sean O'Brien and Corporal Smith might have something to say about our

British expediency on that matter. But let us, Roy, be even more cynical and selfish! We withdraw — then at least we'll not be bringing home any more red, white and blue boxes with working-class mothers' sons in them. Then, if there is the Civil War, the blood bath, it'll only be Catholic and Protestant Paddies ripping each others guts out and we can stand by and say self-righteously: 'See, what the natives do to each other without the English there to rule them!' That's been the *raison d'être* of English colonialism since the world began, Roy. Is that where we're at? The pretence of Peace-Makers! 'We can't have you killing each other. It's messy. We'll do it for you. We're more efficient at it, better practised!'

ROY: But it still does not answer my question, Steven. What about the Protestants? What do we do with them?

STEVEN: O.K. I'll tell you, Roy. Simple. We tell them they're Irish. That we don't want them. And that they're no longer British or Unionist or bloody Loyalist! That's what we do with them. Full stop. End of story!

ELIZABETH: Bravo! Bravo! More! More! Anyone for a brandy?

Hold. Blackout.

15 SCENE

Lights up.
Dublin. A police cell.
We see Liam and Joe.

LIAM: 'Up against the wall and we'll make collanders of you!' That's what he said, Joe.

JOE: So, a Special Branch man is a Special Branch man, no matter whether he talks with a 'brogue', an 'English' accent or like a 'B-Special'. It's hardly surprising, Liam. For they're all tarred with the same brush. At least he was honest. Straight.

LIAM: Oh, he was straight alright. He laid it on the line.

JOE: Which is more than can be said for most of these gombeens in the 26 Counties. Churchill had the Orange card — these fuckers pull out a full pack of Green ones when it suits them. But sure we knew that, Liam. We've known it since '69 with Jack Lynch and his 'not standing idly by'.

LIAM: Aye Joe. I know. But there's a difference between knowing it up here (*taps head*) and coming face to face with it — smack up against it — 'Up against the wall' that's what he said.

JOE: 'In true De Valera fashion'. Well, he was right about that great Celtic myth, wasn't he? For Mr. Eamonn De Valera might have fired guns at the Brits when he was on the corner of Boylan's bakery in 1916, but it didn't stop him executing Republicans when he wanted.

LIAM: Too true, Joe. But you know, the more I think about it, the more I'm convinced we were right.

JOE: About what?

LIAM: About what we were talking about in the room before the raid. We ARE a fuckin' different people, Joe. All Irish? That's a load of fuckin' bullshit. I have as much in common with this shower down here in the South as I have with the man in the moon. We're Northerners first, Joe. And it doesn't matter whether we're Taigs or Prods. And as for the so-called working-class of this 26 Counties bourgeois state, they've given us their answer too.

JOE: And what's that, Liam?

LIAM: 'Fuck off!' Just like Mr. Irish Special Branch man said to me. 'We don't want you and your kind, Liam'. That's what he said!

JOE: But he's not the people of the South, the working class, Liam.

LIAM: Maybe not. But I don't see them rising up in revolutionary solidarity to help us either, Joe. Like our class allies in England, they've WATCHED us fighting for 15 fuckin' years. You can understand it with the English, but you can't excuse these gombeens down here anymore.

JOE: So, it's Unilateral Independence for the Six Counties of Ulster — is that what you're suggesting, Liam?

LIAM: No, Joe. It's not. But what I am saying is that the longer this thing goes on the stronger our Northern identity becomes. People in the North have no friends and that's true for us Taigs as well as the Prods. We have none in the South and the Prods have none in England.

JOE: Tell that to the Loyalists and Paisley!

LIAM: Oh, it's dawning on them, Joe. They're beginning to get the message.

JOE: And in the meantime, while they're making up their minds, they're bumping off Taigs left right and centre.

LIAM: I'm not making excuses for them, Joe. Though mind you, there's a few down here in the South I'd give them a helping hand with.

JOE: Liam, do you realize what you're saying?

LIAM: Aye, Joe. I think I do. For what I'm saying is that the Prods, the Loyalists, deep down in their hearts know the game's up. That 'one day' the Brits are going to leave. They know they're going to be sold down the river, just like the South sold us out, and it's when the Brits DO leave the North that the real fun in Ireland starts. The time'll have come then for us 'Northern Taigs' and 'Northern Prods' and our 'Northern Troubles' to really spill over the border. And with the hardware we have amongst us, it'll be the Southern gombeens who'll be up against the wall.

JOE: Hordes of Nor ʻrn invaders descending upon Dublin and Galway and C   , Liam!

Enter masked figure. Sound of explosion.

FIGURE: Right, comrades. C'mon. It's a break-out. C'mon. Hurry it up.

Blackout. Music.

Lights up.
The Bishop's residence.
We see Father Crilly again standing by the window as he was in the
first scene in Bishop's sitting room.
Silence.
Enter Bishop looking very pleased.

BISHOP: Well, Father Crilly, what a turn-up for the books that
was. Don't you think?

FATHER CRILLY: It was a SURPRISE alright, Your Eminence.

BISHOP: I told you he was bright, Father Crilly. Oh, our Father
Quinn is no fool, and that's for sure. I only wish a few more
of our young curates displayed such a degree of insight AND
FORESIGHT!

FATHER CRILLY: Yes, Your Eminence. He does seem to think
ahead.

BISHOP: Think ahead, is it? You're becoming a master of
understatement, Father Crilly. What Father Quinn said
was tantamount to brilliance. And he never gave you an
indication of what his real thoughts were on the matter,
Father Crilly? His tactics? Strategy?

FATHER CRILLY: No. Your Eminence. He did not. But perhaps I
was wrong in the way I dealt with it. Too much of a jumping
to conclusions on my part. The old Parish priest, you know,
disliking and feeling threatened by what I saw as the
'modernism' of the new young 'popular' priest in the
parish.

BISHOP: Oh, I wouldn't feel too bad about it, Father Crilly. For I, myself, in the discussions we've had about and with Father Quinn, had jumped also to that same conclusion. The 'avant-garde' young upstart — thinking ONLY HE knew about life and Church politics! Ah, so we were both a little wrong, but no matter now that we know what he's up to and perhaps what he said is thought-provoking for us all.

FATHER CRILLY: It is that, Your Eminence. And, although I reacted with incredulity when he was explaining himself, I was just thinking there, as I looked out of your window again and up at the Cave Hill, that this land of ours does have a bewitching pagan quality about it. Did you know, Your Eminence, that on the other side of that hill there is a spot where, as the story goes, a witch did live? I remember the story from my mother telling it, and a better Catholic you couldn't meet. And that on that spot, the site where this witch lived, today there is a British Army post. And, on that same Cave Hill, there is a place where a meeting of Wolfe Tone and the United Irishmen occurred. They were planning the '98 Rebellion which was Protestant inspired as you know, Your Eminence — and then there's MacArts Fort and. . .

BISHOP: Yes, Father Crilly. There's more than just the scenic beauty to look at from that window.

FATHER CRILLY: Aye, Your Eminence. There is. And our Father Quinn would seem to be right in taking it all into some kind of perspective, for what we're dealing with may not be as simple or straightforward as we sometimes allow ourselves to think.

BISHOP: Nothing ever is, Father Crilly. But Mother Church is an old hand at dealing with things simple or complex, and I think she can handle this one too. Father Quinn has maybe given us a new lever. The world is a strange place these days, Father Crilly, and it maybe seems even stranger to us, who were brought up in a world where the tactics and strategy of a Father Quinn were not necessary.

FATHER CRILLY: So, you think Father Quinn should continue with the newspaper column then, Your Eminence?

BISHOP: I do, Father Crilly. And I think he should be listened to carefully. We'll still keep a close check on how things develop, mind you, but if he's achieving what we want him to achieve — that is, what is good for the Church and Catholicism in Ireland and especially here in the North — then we'll not stand in his way or be prohibitive. And you said he was popular, Father Crilly?

FATHER CRILLY: Oh, he is that, Your Eminence. With old and young alike. They see him as a 'priest of the people'.

BISHOP: And if he manages, Father Crilly, to take away some of the influence of those others among our community who have appointed themselves as the people's voice, then WE are still winning the battle for minds and souls. Are we not, Father Crilly?

FATHER CRILLY: I certainly hope so, Your Eminence. For the challengers have been vociferous in recent times.

BISHOP: As they have been before, Father Crilly. But with men like Father Quinn around, I think you can be sure that we'll hold our own. It'll take more than a few half-educated revolutionaries to overcome and defeat the men of Maynooth! Now, will you be staying to lunch, Father Crilly? For, if you are, I'd better be letting my housekeeper know, otherwise we will really have trouble and rebellion on our hands!

FATHER CRILLY: No, I won't, Your Eminence, thank you all the same. I must get back to the parish. I have a meeting with the builders over lunch, about the school. Normal parish business must proceed as well.

BISHOP: Very true, Father Crilly. But you'll have a drink before you go. Whiskey?

FATHER CRILLY: A small one, then, Your Eminence. Thank you.

Drinks business.

BISHOP: Well, here's to Father Quinn and his Andersonstown News!

Both drink. Hold.
Slow fade. Music.

17 | SCENE

Lights up.
Belfast. We see Frankie, last seen in scene 3.
She is sitting reading 'Republican News'.
Silence.

Enter Liam

Liam looks tired, dirty and bruised.

FRANKIE: What the fuck are you doing here?

LIAM: Irish hospitality, as usual. Eh, Frankie? What the fuck does it look like. I'm 'on the run' from the South . . . the 'Republic' (*he laughs*).

FRANKIE: Never mind the wise-cracks, Liam. What happened?

LIAM: You mean YOU haven't heard. I know there's censorship, Frankie but . . .

FRANKIE: I don't mean that. I heard about the breakout. I mean afterwards.

LIAM: They chased us!

FRANKIE: Oh, very fuckin' funny, Liam. You'd be smiling on the other side of your face if they'd caught you.

LIAM: Thanks. Maybe I would. But they didn't. I don't know about the rest, though. Has there been any news?
Pause.

FRANKIE: They picked up Joe. And the others.

LIAM: Fuck them! The gombeen bastards!

FRANKIE: But what happened? How did you get here?

LIAM: Oh, never mind that now, Frankie. Just start believing in miracles. I'm here. And you're gonna have to sort out what to do with me.

FRANKIE: Aye. Well, we'll maybe have to try and get you out of the country. Hope that things stay quiet for a few days and then shift you.

LIAM: You want to know something, Frankie? I think I'd nearly prefer to get picked up here.

FRANKIE: What are you talking about?

LIAM: No. Seriously. That's why I came back. I've been thinking about it. I thought about it all fuckin' night after I got away and was holed up in this aul shack I came across. I had one single aim — not to get picked up on the Southern side of the border. And you wanna know something else, Frankie? When I realized I was in the North, I screamed for joy. I was going to go looking for a Brit patrol, or an R.U.C. police station and say — 'Here I am, put me in Long Kesh, please'.

FRANKIE: What's wrong with you, Liam? Have you taken leave of your senses?

LIAM: No, Frankie. I've only just got sense.

FRANKIE: What the hell are you on about?

LIAM: Well, I'll tell you, Frankie. If I get picked up here in the North — or maybe I should say 'when' — I'll get put in the Kesh.

Frankie looks at him almost stunned.

LIAM: And the Kesh is full of the lads, Northern lads.

FRANKIE: Yeh.

LIAM: And the warders are mostly Orangemen or ex-'B' Specials, or both, who want to kick fuck out of us Fenians.

FRANKIE: They'll want to AND do it, Liam!

LIAM: Yeh. Well, Frankie, I'd prefer THEM to do it than some big fat ham-faced Southern Catholic from Kerry or Dublin. It would be easier to take — cope with. For in a black Protestant twisted way it has a kind of logic. But there's no fuckin' logic to a gombeen Southerner, Frankie. And that's who would be doing it if I got picked up in the South. And

I'm not sure if I'd be able to handle that, Frankie. For they'd probably have to kill me — for that's what I'd want to do to them. So, Frankie, when we get rid of the Brits, don't be putting the guns away, for we'll need every last one of them, and more, to DEAL with the enemy within. North against South, Frankie.

VOICE OF BRITISH
SOLDIER/LOUDHAILER: This is Sergeant Wilson speaking. We have the place surrounded. Come out slowly with your hands on your head. You, first, Liam Doherty.

Liam turns, almost smiling. Hold. Blackout.

18 | SCENE

London. A police cell.
We see Derek and Wee Johnny, a Belfast Tramp/Wino.
Wee Johnny sings song (She Moves Through the Fair) as lights slowly come up. Finishes song.

JOHNNY: Women, son — they can be a man's downfall. Mind you, I had been damn near counted out before. You see, the trouble was, she kept trying to put me on my feet, well, they couldn't take the weight you see (*he chuckles*). But could I convince her? (*shakes head*) Your first time inside, son? I can tell it is by the expression on your face, it has that 'Is this really me in here?' look about it. But after the first time you never have that expression ever again. It's never as innocent again. Not after you've been in here ONCE! The name's Gilmore, son, Johnny Gilmore, but I'm known as Wee Johnny, to do with my height only, not the size of anything else, not that that matters these days or for a long time past. And what should I be calling you, son?

Pause.

DEREK: Derek. Derek Smith.

JOHNNY: And with an accent like that you must be a Belfast man like myself.

DEREK: Aye. I'm from Belfast.

JOHNNY: (*Smiling*) Your name would seem to indicate to me, though, that you kick with the wrong foot. Would I be right?

DEREK: (*Smiles knowingly*) But maybe it's you kicks with the wrong foot, Wee Johnny!

JOHNNY: Maybe we both do . . . if we're in here.

DEREK: Aye. Well, you're probably RIGHT about that.

JOHNNY: So, you're a Sweeney Todd, Derek.

DEREK: And you must be a Taig, Johnny.

JOHNNY: Well, that didn't take long and we didn't even have to get to the 'what school did you go to' bit.

DEREK: (*Laughing*) Or where abouts in Belfast are you from?

JOHNNY: Oh, I always answer WEST BELFAST to that one.

DEREK: So do I.

JOHNNY: Shankill Road?

Derek nods.

DEREK: Falls?

Johnny nods.

JOHNNY: Parallel lines: the distance of a spit from each other and yet worlds apart.

DEREK: I wonder how many English people know just how close the Shankill and Falls are. Physically, I mean.

JOHNNY: None too many I would think, and what's more, they couldn't care less, Derek.

DEREK: Oh, you're right there, Johnny. I'm beginning to see that for myself.

JOHNNY: Oh, I've always been of the opinion, Derek, that our fellow country men of both Churches, so to speak, should be forced to spend time together in England on a regular basis.

DEREK: It would be a revelation to a lot of them, Johnny.

JOHNNY: Revelation? It would be the cause of a fuckin' revolution, Derek, that's what it would be. Revolution — throughout the whole of the fuckin' Disunited Kingdom. And if enough of them came and saw, then they could spread the word to the Welsh and the Scottish, not forgetting the Cornish!

DEREK: And how long have you yourself been across the water, Johnny?

JOHNNY: Me? Here? Oh, a long time. I came over first in '39. Then the war broke out and, like manys another Paddy, I took pot shots at Hitler — sang God Save Churchill. The war ended, I got a kick in the bollocks for my troubles, went home to Ireland, couldn't get a job and, to tell you the truth, I couldn't stand the place or the people either. So I went into exile again: became a hungry fighter, made a few bob; kicked the gong around for a while; married; became unmarried; clashed with a younger hungrier fighter — then I retired. I've been retired now 28 years. I was one of the first to take early retirement. I'd recommend it, Derek. Working's only for those who don't know how to spend their time.

DEREK: But if you have the time and no money, what then, Johnny?

JOHNNY: Have you ever heard the phrase 'Property is Theft'. It was a book written by a Russian fellow, name of Proud One . . .

DEREK: I've heard the saying, Johnny.

JOHNNY: Well, I'm the Theft of the title and places like this are the Property. And now and again Property catches up on me. Well, here I am — this is one of those times. But what about yourself, son. Why are you a guest in Property's Halls?

DEREK: An accident.

JOHNNY: An accident? Ah, now you're coding me — for there's no such thing as an accident, Derek. Everything has its reason. It's trying to find it — the reason — is the problem.

DEREK: No, Johnny. You don't understand. It was an accident at work — on the site.

JOHNNY: Building site? What happened?

DEREK: Well, to cut a long story short, the foreman had a go at me, took a swing at me in fact. I tripped him, he hit his head on an iron girder and he's on the danger list in hospital.

JOHNNY: Ssssssh! Tricky!

DEREK: You're fuckin' right, Johnny. And that bastardin' Detective was getting very tricky. Starting asking me about political organizations at home and was I a LOYALIST? And the way he said it! 'Are you what some might call a LOYALIST, Mr Smith?'

JOHNNY: You mean he said 'LOYALIST' the way you might say 'FENIAN'.

DEREK: Yeh. (*Pause*). I see what you mean, Johnny. I take your point.

JOHNNY: 'LOYALIST'. 'FENIAN'. It's all the same to him, Derek. Just different ways of saying 'PADDY'. Ah, we might think we're different tribes to each other, but to an English detective we're all the one band of NATIVES.

DEREK: All branded the same once we step off that Liverpool boat.

JOHNNY: That's it, Derek. Exactly.

DEREK: You know, Johnny, that's what I was saying to my mate one night, before all this business happened. My mate laughed it off and made a crack about me talking like a Taig. But you know, Johnny, I'm thinking, the reason why he tried to laugh it off — why he didn't want to talk about it, face it — is: it's hard for us to face. Harder for us to be called a PADDY than, say, you, Johnny. For we thought we were different: we thought we were like them, we were British. LOYALISTS, Johnny. And what's happening is that what we were LOYAL to . . . doesn't want us . . . despises us. And it's hard, Johnny, it's fuckin' hard to take. For we're out on a limb and we've no friends — neither Irish nor British — and we're scared, Johnny. We're fuckin' scared!

Enter Detective.

JOHNNY: Oh, hello there, Detective. And how's business down at the Yard?

DETECTIVE: He's dead, Mr. Smith.

Hold/slow fade.
Music.

The London Flat.
Elizabeth, Roy and Steven are now back in the lounge having brandies.
Lights up.

ELIZABETH: Cheers, comrades!

ROY AND STEVEN: Cheers, Elizabeth.

ELIZABETH: I thoroughly enjoyed that, Steven. The short speech of solution about the Ulster Protestants. Excellent stuff!

ROY: I don't think you were exactly meant to enjoy it, Elizabeth. I don't think entertainment was Steven's purpose, was it comrade?

STEVEN: Hmm. Well . . . ah . . .

ELIZABETH: Roy! Just for once . . . Fuck off and pour me another brandy, comrade.

ROY: Elizabeth . . .

Roy shocked and embarrassed spills brandy.

ELIZABETH: Roy, please don't spill it. I want to enjoy it as much as I can before your lot get into power and increase the tax on it as a non-working class, right-off luxury!

ROY: Elizabeth, are you feeling well?

ELIZABETH: Yes. Perfect. Thank you, Roy. It's just I've listened all evening like a little obedient woman to you and Steve and I feel it's now time to exercise my own little female tongue — if that's O.K., of course, comrades.

STEVEN: Elizabeth. I am sorry. We have been very rude and thoughtless, Roy. You know we two do go on a bit at times.

ROY: Yes. I expect we do, Steven. Apologies, Elizabeth.

ELIZABETH: No. Please. Don't apologize. Politeness is the last refuge of a white male bourgeois liberal and you, boys, wouldn't want to be called that.

ROY: We'd accept the male part, Elizabeth.

ELIZABETH: Really?

STEVEN: I think maybe I better be going, Roy.

ELIZABETH: No, Steven. We wouldn't dream of letting you leave so early. And you don't really want to go without hearing my little vocal offering of the evening.

STEVEN: Well, perhaps . . . and it is still quite early.

ROY: Let me top you up, Steven.

Drinks business.

ELIZABETH: You mustn't think I was taking the piss, Steven, when I said I enjoyed what you said about Northern Ireland's protestants.

STEVEN: No offence was taken, Elizabeth. Why, do you agree with what I said?

ELIZABETH: No. Not in the slightest, Steven. But it was the passion and commitment with which you said it that I enjoyed. To witness an English man, an English politician, an English socialist, speak with such intensity and the hint of a raised voice can come close to making a woman's heart flutter. You know, I've often thought that if the Irish were more like the English man and the English man were more like the Irish, the balance of passion and reason might be at a more satisfactory keel. But no, I think you are wrong in your analysis. I think you are both wrong.

ROY: And why is that, Elizabeth?

ELIZABETH: Well, I shall tell you why if you will permit, Roy.

STEVEN: Let us two listen a bit, Roy. For I am interested in what Elizabeth has to say.

ROY: Of course, comrade. Let's listen then.

ELIZABETH: Thank you, gentlemen.

Pause.

ELIZABETH: Well. Let me tell you what really pisses me off about you men of the English Left — and this is blatant sexism aside — but I find you stupid or at very best naive.

ROY: Elizabeth, I don't think it's necessary to be so rude!

ELIZABETH: Your capacities, comrades, for analysis of a very complex political and cultural conundrum are immensely limited. Being professional politicians you are tremendously susceptible to the whims of fashion.

And it is the fashion at present amongst the English Left to support Troops Out of Ireland and make the right-on revolutionary gestures of sympathy towards the I.R.A. In fact, it could be said that you come in your y-fronts with excitement at the thought of being associated with the Northern Irish men and women of real revolutionary violence. The English revolution is not happening on the streets of London, or Liverpool, or Manchester but, God, isn't it thrilling to feel sympathy with, meet, talk to, someone who may have used a real gun? Or if they haven't, then they certainly know some one who has. Revolution . . . three . . . four persons removed.

ROY: Elizabeth, I think maybe you've said enough for now. . .

ELIZABETH: Also, you're full of the worst kind of patronizing liberal guilt. Guilt about the Blacks, the Asians, the Serbo-Croatians, the Palestinians and the Irish in Ireland. Ireland! England's — our — oldest colony! Poor Patricks and Brigids! Well, let me tell you some thing about the North of Ireland, the wee six counties of Ulster — and I speak now as a professional historian, observer of contemporary events and mainland witness to the last 15 years of civil strife —.

Far from being single-mindedly big bad Britannia, England has been, more times than the likes of you unthinking sloganizers would care to consider, a paragon of virtue and patience regarding the Anglo-Irish quagmire. Tell me, where else, in what earthly space, do you find neo-Celtic paganism, Roman Catholicism of a type guaranteed to give even the Poles nightmares, and seventeenth century Calvinism of a form that would have Calvin himself shit-scared, all mixed up together and seeping through in one gigantic enormous black pot of Irish Stew? Where else? Nowhere else, comrades. But it is that stew which lies thick and crustating in the minds and psyches of the people who inhabit the wee six counties of the political entity known as Northern Bloody Ireland. And it is that stew-pot that we, the English, dangle round our guilt-ridden necks like an occult milestone!

ROY: This is outrageous. Are you drunk, woman? Steve, I'm terribly sorry about this.

Elizabeth refills all glasses.

ELIZABETH: For you see, gentlemen, British involvement in Ireland can no longer be simplistically labelled as old-fashioned imperialism. It is not that we need to Paddy-bash to reaffirm the healthy state of our Anglo-Saxon mentalities, but, as someone once said: 'Looked at with English eyes, Ireland is the end of the world; to the Irish, glazed with the glory of Celtic Christendom, it is the centre of Atlantic Europe.' But to a late twentieth century, modern Government's eyes, that island of Erin at the end of the world is today an open route and gateway for an Eastern nuclear attack. And that centre of Atlantic Europe is today glazed with the frosty breath of East/West world politics. Yes, comrades, the truth is, we shall be in Ireland for some long time to come, maybe a very, very long time, maybe until the world and its people decide to arrange their affairs very, very differently. Until then, irrespective of whether it is 26 and six or just one job lot of 32, we will have our presence in Ireland!

Blackout/but in blackout we see backdrop of world map with flickering pin-heads (indicative of world military strategic positions).
Hold this effect/then cut all other flickering pin-heads except the one in Ireland.
Hold briefly.
Total blackout/music.